So You Want to Write a Screenplay

A Step-by-Step Guide to Writing for Film, Video, and Television

By Taylor Gaines

Foreword by Max Timm, Director of
Community Outreach with the International
Screenwriters' Association (ISA)

So You Want to Write a Screenplay:
A Step-by-Step Guide to Writing for Film, Video, and Television

Website: www.atlantic-pub.com • Email: sales@atlantic-pub.com
SAN Number: 268-1250

Library of Congress Cataloging-in-Publication Data

Names: Gaines, Taylor.
Title: So you want to write a screenplay : a step-by-step guide to writing
    for film, video, and television / by Taylor Gaines.
Description: Ocala, Florida : Atlantic Publishing Group, Inc., 2016. |
    Includes bibliographical references and index.
Identifiers: LCCN 2016035474| ISBN 9781620232156 (pbk. : alk. paper) | ISBN
    9781620232590 (library) | ISBN 1620232154
Subjects: LCSH: Motion picture authorship. | Motion picture
    authorship--Vocational guidance. | Television authorship. | Television
    authorship--Vocational guidance.
Classification: LCC PN1996 .G285 2016 | DDC 808.2/3--dc23 LC record available at https://lccn.loc.gov/
2016035474

PROJECT MANAGER AND EDITOR: Rebekah Sack – rsack@atlantic-pub.com
INTERIOR LAYOUT AND JACKET DESIGN: Janine Milstrey – contact@red-cape.de
COVER DESIGN: Jackie Miller – sullmill@charter.net

Printed in the United States

Over the years, we have adopted a number of dogs from rescues and shelters. First there was Bear and after he passed, Ginger and Scout. Now, we have Kira, another rescue. They have brought immense joy and love not just into our lives, but into the lives of all who met them.

We want you to know a portion of the profits of this book will be donated in Bear, Ginger and Scout's memory to local animal shelters, parks, conservation organizations, and other individuals and nonprofit organizations in need of assistance.

— Douglas & Sherri Brown,
President & Vice-President of Atlantic Publishing

TABLE OF CONTENTS

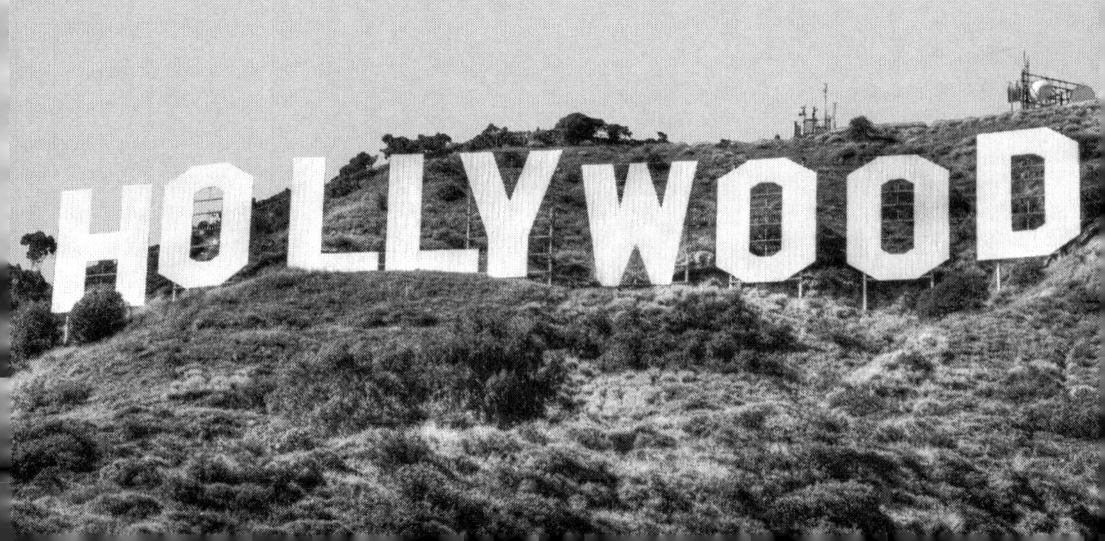

Table of Contents	4
Foreword	9
Introduction	13
Screenwriting 101	15
Screenwriting as a Teen	17
Chapter 1:	
What Makes a Great Screenwriter	21
Qualities	23
Writing Commitment	27
Fiction vs. Nonfiction	29
Chapter 2:	37
Learning From the Pros	37
Reading Screenwriting Online	39
Watching and Analyzing Movies	43
Watching Foreign Films	52
Chapter 3:	
Getting Started: Focusing on Your Story	59
Research	61
Genre	66
Setting Your Idea Apart	68
Creating Characters	69
Writing Scenes	77

Chapter 4:   93
Storytelling 101   93
  Character Development   95
  Writing to Help Understand Your Characters 101
  Creating Structure   103
  Creating an Outline   119
  Establishing Voice   127

Chapter 5:
Beginnings and Endings   137
  The Beginning   139
  The MacGuffin   141
  Ending   142

Chapter 6:
Developing Theme   147
  How to Develop Theme   151
  Symbolic Elements   155

Chapter 7:
Look Like a Pro — Formatting and Revisions   161
  Screenwriting Software   163
  Formatting   164
  Feedback   167
  Rewriting   170

Chapter 8:
Become a Marketing Expert   179
   Copyright   181
   Researching the Market   184
   The Sale Process   186
   Example of query letter   189

Chapter 9:
Get Your Script on the Screen   195
   Networking   197
   Independent Films   199
   Short Films   201
   Student Films   203

Conclusion   204
Bibliography   206
Glossary   208

Additional Resources   212
   Sample Scripts   213
   About Screenwriting   213
   Hollywood and the Business   214
   Working Screenwriters and Industry Insiders   215
   Downloads   216

Index   218
Author Bio   222

FOREWORD

The only true currency in the business of screenwriting is uniqueness. Let go of the intention to make a bushel of money — that can happen, and if you put in the time and have a little bit of luck on your side, it will happen. It's more important, however, to focus on the essentials and fundamentals in order to align yourself with the energy of the *process* of writing. Most, if not all, of your time is spent hunched over a notebook or laptop clicking away at a keyboard or scribbling notes. Very little of your time as a writer is spent basking in success, red carpet events, or hob-knobbing with the entertainment elite.

The fun and excitement of the writing process is and should always be found through work and time. So, by saying you should "align yourself with the energy of the process of writing," I mean that every writer needs to continually focus on educating him or herself and revel in the quiet excitement of creating a story. You are a storyteller at heart, otherwise you wouldn't be reading this book, but every storyteller — regardless of his or her level of mastery — is constantly on the hunt for the next and more enticing adventure. It is, however, absolutely necessary for every writer to start at the beginning, and just like a professional athlete, focus on the fundamentals and perfect the fundamentals, before he or she ever expects to become a professional.

By perfecting the fundamentals of not only the writing process, but also the storytelling process, you will quite quickly discover your own personal voice, and therefore your unique approach to entertaining the masses. You are the only one who can tell the story you have in your head, and that makes you and your writing process special and unique. Take pride in that.

By picking up this book, you have made the decision to focus on the process, and because of that decision, you are already two steps ahead of the writer who believes he can do it on his own. Enjoy the process. Take it one step at a time. And allow your unique self to shine every step of the way.

— Max Timm

Max Timm is the Director of Community Outreach with the International Screenwriters' Association (ISA) and the author of the award-winning YA fantasy, The WishKeeper.

INTRODUCTION

Today, stars are being made everywhere. YouTube. Vine. Vimeo. Snapchat. But if you picked up this book, you're someone who realizes there's still nothing quite like getting your work put up on the big screen. Writing movies is not easy, but it remains arguably the most rewarding way to have your work recognized. Television is also fast approaching in prestige and popularity with more than 400 original scripted television series on television in 2015 alone. It's a bit of a different ecosystem, but the general storytelling techniques and methods are similar in some ways, too.

The pay isn't going to be anything like that of a movie star — A-listers like Meryl Streep and Denzel Washington can make between $5 million and $20 million per movie — but it's still a pretty good chunk of cash (Siegemund-Broka and Bond, 2015). Typically, screenwriters — even a first-time one — will get between two and five percent of a movie's total budget for the screenplay, according to the Writers' Guild of Great Britain (2016). The average wide-release movie costs $65 million according to the Motion Picture Association of America (2007). That means you have the potential to bring in $3.25 million from one script!

SCREENWRITING 101

You've probably become numb to how much a single line of dialogue in a movie or TV show script actually accomplishes. The words on the page are just the tip of the iceberg.

Think about it — words have to create and convey a world, a mindset, a history, motivations, plot, and much more.

For example, take a family drama like *August: Osage County* (2013) or *The Fighter* (2010). The screenwriter has to know the quirks and habits of the family and its interactions. Think of the way your mom always flinches when someone mentions your family trip to Disney World, or the way your dad always uses the word *literally* when there's nothing literal about the situation. It's things like that that writers have to make note of and show through dialogue so that characters can resonate with the audience.

Research and planning is important as well. When a movie is grounded in reality, the writer has to be intimately familiar with the time period, the speech patterns of the time, the details of a character's job, and countless other things. It can take viewers out of the movie very quickly if something is inaccurate.

Even in fictional universes like *The Matrix* (1999) or *Avatar* (2009), the screenwriter has to create rules for his or her fictional world and stick to them. Thoroughly planning and researching your story is key.

Your script is not just about the words that make up the story. It's about the images. Movies have to resonate with you visually.

Think of how you might describe your house to someone. You wouldn't want to say that it's a "brownstone Victorian-style house with green trim; one story and a two-car garage." You'd want to describe it as it resonates in your head. "It's the one with the big maple tree in front of it and the American flag waving from the garage."

The words you choose should be impactful and descriptive while also keeping your script as concise as possible.

SCREENWRITING AS A TEEN

I get it. You're busy with school, sports, friends, video games, and whatever else takes up your days. And this sounds like a lot of work. How can you have time to write a screenplay?

Know this: It is a lot of work, and it will take a lot of time. But when you have a screenplay to call your own before you graduate college (or even high school), you'll be glad you made the effort.

The easiest thing to do is to set aside a particular amount of time each day where you will work on your screenplay. Make it a routine. Write 30 minutes every day after school. Whatever works for you. Some days, you might write thousands of words. Some days, you might write none.

Your idea might be small at first. What if dogs could speak and hold positions of power in the government? What if having more than one child was illegal? What if time didn't exist? Your idea might be fruitful, and it might not be. The only way you can know is by writing.

The best thing to do is to write whatever is in your head first and think about refining and re-writing later. You'll have to expand, re-search, and outline your idea before the process is up if you want a coherent and cohesive screenplay.

This guide will give you the lowdown on the entire screenwriting process. Knowing the ins and outs of the business will give you a leg up on your competition. In this book, every aspect of the script-writing process is covered, from your initial idea to pitching your screenplay to agents and executives.

So sit down, buckle up, and get ready to write a screenplay! But first, let's get inspired.

Celeste Davis

Celeste Davis is a lover of writing.

"When you enjoy something, you just do it without even thinking about it," she says. "My passion is writing."

For Celeste, the trick to getting a screenplay done was simple: Just write it.

Like many teenagers, she felt out of place among her peers when she entered her teens. She didn't know what it took to fit in and didn't particularly care to find out. She took her frustrations out by writing a story called *Purgatory House*, where a teenager is faced with a series of decisions after committing suicide and awaking in the afterlife. It was turned into a feature film by the time she was 14 years old and wound up on five critics' lists for best film of the year.

"I didn't have any discipline in my life until I started making this movie," she said. "I also now know that there really is joy and happiness — you just have to find the strength and motivation to create what you want."

Steven Spielberg

Steven Spielberg got turned down from the University of Southern California film school. You know the name, right? He's only one of the most successful and prolific movie directors of all-time. *Jaws* (1975), *Jurassic Park* (1993), *Saving Private Ryan* (1998), *E.T.* (1982)... the list goes on.

When he applied to USC in the 1960s, Spielberg was turned down because of his "C" grade average. He wound up attending (and dropping out of) California State University, Long Beach, to make a short film named *Amblin'* (1968).

I guess test scores don't tell you everything. Even if you don't have immediate success, hard work and talent can pay off in the long run.

Spielberg bet on himself, and he won. He has gone on to be nominated for 16 Academy Awards, winning Best Director for *Saving Private Ryan* and *Schindler's List* (1993). His movies have grossed more than $4 billion in his lifetime.

CHAPTER 1:

WHAT MAKES
A GREAT
SCREENWRITER

Being a screenwriter is about a lot more than just writing. Yes, you need to know how to write, and yes, that's still the most important part of the job. But, there are many other qualities that make up a good writer.

QUALITIES

Let's take a look at some of the skills that go into being a successful screenwriter.

Curiosity

Why are we here? What is our life's purpose? What is true love? These are the kinds of questions that float through the heads of screenwriters. They are just people searching for answers to life's questions.

It might help to be someone who thinks about things in a curious way, too. *Wait, why aren't we allowed to chew gum in class? Do I really have to ask my teacher to use the restroom? Why can't we use our phones in class?* If you are constantly questioning things, you might just be a writer.

ASK THE EXPERT: "If it can be written, or thought, it can be filmed."
— Stanley Kubrick, filmmaker, and 13-time Academy Award nominee

Research skills

Thanks to the internet, audiences can check the accuracy of even the smallest fact in your movie. This makes it harder and harder to get viewers to suspend disbelief and go on your film's journey. Your ability to research online, in books, and through other critical fact-finding sources will help you a great deal as a writer in avoiding these mistakes.

Details

Your character can't just have a dog. Your character has to have a golden retriever named Skippy. Details are critical to making your story pop, and you'll find that the most successful screenwriters are very detail-oriented. For images to resonate with people, they have to be as specific as possible. The saying "show don't tell" is a good one to remember as you write.

Let's say that one of your main character's traits is that he is nervous around others. Don't simply say, "He walked around nervously." Use your character's actions to show the nerves. For example, "He pulled at his shirt constantly; he kept his hands in his pockets; he kept playing with his hair." Don't be afraid to get creative and specific.

ASK THE EXPERT: "Making people believe the unbelievable is no trick; it's work... belief and reader absorption come in the details: An overturned tricycle in the gutter of an abandoned neighborhood can stand for everything."
      – Stephen King, author whose books have inspired many movies and television shows

Brevity
When you are writing a movie, you have to question what is and what isn't necessary for the story to ensure it has as little fat on it as possible. Is there anything worse than a bad movie that's also way too long? Screenwriters have to work in a more confined space than, say, a novelist. Extra words have no place in a script.

Flexibility
As a writer, you have to learn how to swallow your pride. In trying to sell a script and get a movie made, you will have to learn how to accept feedback in order to make your script stronger. This may mean an entire re-write, cutting certain scenes, or changing characters. This can be a hard thing to adjust to, but it's the nature of being a writer.

ASK THE EXPERT: "If it sounds like writing, I rewrite it."

— Elmore Leonard, author whose books have inspired many movies and television shows

Dedication

Writing and rewriting your script can be a tedious and lonely process. Even once you finish your script, there is a lot of work to be done in researching agents, preparing treatments and manuscripts, entering contests, and working on marketing tools like short films and websites. Are you prepared for all of the hard work?

Vision

In the movies, the final vision is often credited to the director. It's impossible to make a film without a screenwriter, though. A good screenwriter needs to be able to craft a vivid image and strong characters. This might mean writing detailed backgrounds and biographies for characters, even if that information doesn't make it into the script. Some writers sketch out floor plans of homes and locations in the script to help them better visualize things.

As you work on your craft, you will see these skills continue to develop and improve. You will grow more and more comfortable with the writing process. You will also discover many other qualities that can assist you in your writing. This is by no means an exclusive list.

WRITING COMMITMENT

Don't let yourself mythologize writers. Even successful ones have times where they struggle to write. It's not a magical process where shooting stars come out of your fingers and you type up an entirely beautiful and elegant script on the first try.

You probably know someone who walks around claiming they are writing a screenplay with no evidence that they are actually doing so. Many people fall in love with the idea and never get around to executing it.

One of the reasons it's difficult to finish a screenplay is because it can be hard to stay focused and committed when your work is not producing the same results every day. If you're working out, for example, that's easy. You run on the treadmill for 30 minutes, and you burn a certain amount of calories. With writing, be warned: results may vary.

One day, you may write 1,500 words in an hour. The next, you might get inspired and write 3,000. Then, writer's block may hit, and you'll only write 500 words the next day. It's easy to get frustrated by this fluctuating output, and you may want to quit.

The more you sit down and write, though, the more consistent you'll get. Just stay committed. Sit down for a set amount of time every day, and get it done.

Get inspired

Writers should always be writing. As you go about your day, you should be thinking about your screenplay. Let it soak into every part of your life. You'll find that things that happen in your daily life make their way into your script or inspire parts of it.

One thing you could try is keeping a notebook with you at all times in case inspiration strikes. Having one or two sentences or ideas written down can help you avoid writer's block and keep your flow going. If you don't feel like going old school with a handheld notebook, use the notepad function on your phone to serve the same purpose.

Don't get lonely

It can be really hard to make yourself sit down in a quiet place to write every day when your friends are busy having fun. Being alone might be necessary for you to do productive writing, but it does not have to be a completely solitary experience.

Try building a network of writer friends so that you have someone who will read your work and give you honest feedback. If you feel like you are drowning in a project, it can be very helpful to have someone not involved with it to give you some perspective.

If you are enrolled in a creative writing class, there will most likely be times when you can get critiqued on your work. Most writing classes do a dedicated workshop for the students — you might be able to pass around your tentative first draft there. If not, you can always email teachers and ask for advice: "Would you be willing to take a look at this draft, and if not, could you possibly point me to someone that could? Perhaps a writing group exists that I don't know about?"

Even asking a friend or parent who doesn't seem interested in moviemaking can be useful. It helps to know what an average person thinks of your story as well. Stories are the way humans interact, so they are bound to have some thoughts (though you might not want to listen to all of them).

Stay strong

At the beginning, you may be very excited about working on your script. You'll tell everyone you know about it and think about it constantly. As the process begins to require more time and effort, though, you may struggle to stay focused. The writing may begin to feel like a slog. At this critical moment, you have to push through and keep working.

Writing cannot just be a hobby or something you do in your spare time. It has to become a habit. If it's not part of your daily routine to sit down and write, you will probably struggle to get your screenplay done. Tell your family and friends not to disturb you during your writing time. Download a program like *Freedom* or *Write or Die* that will block internet use when you're supposed to be writing. Focus.

FICTION VS. NONFICTION

Whether you are writing fiction or nonfiction stories, it's going to take a lot of work and preparation. Let's take a quick look at each approach.

Fiction writers

The key to a fictional screenplay is telling your story in the most concise and powerful manner possible. You have less room to roam than if you were writing a novel, so you have to come prepared. Working on a fictional screenplay without outlining first is a recipe for disaster.

> ASK THE EXPERT: "All readers come to fiction as willing accomplices to your lies. Such is the basic goodwill contract made the moment we pick up a work of fiction."
> – Steve Almond, short-story writer, essayist and author of 10 books

You also have to make sure to research your subject. Even in fiction, people will be quick to jump on things that come across as unrealistic or unbelievable. You have to be prepared to set rules and laws for your fictional world.

Nonfiction writers

Nonfiction writing is typically a showcase for all of the research that a writer has done. But you are still telling a story, so that research has to be woven into the script more carefully.

For example, let's say your story takes place in a growing town of hip, young professionals. You can't just tell people in words what the town is like. Remember: show, don't tell. You have to convey the aesthetic of the town using images, character traits, or clothing. Screenwriting in nonfiction is all about revealing the right information in the margins to help the audience understand the setting.

CASE STUDY:
WRITING FOR TELEVISION

Jason Klamm
Writer, Director, and Actor
www.stolendress.com
Twitter: @jklamm

We live in an age where TV and film are starting to look and feel very similar to one another. It used to be a lot easier to tell someone how to write for television versus writing for film. The big difference, still, even if you're writing for a TV show that looks as beautiful and scenic and epic as your average film, is scope and scale. This is the case even when you're writing comedy, which happens to be my specialty.

When you're writing for film, you're looking at a single story with a through-line that will last three acts (usually), following the development of a character or group of characters during that story. Sure, you'll have subplots in a film, but they all have to connect to the main plotline, they all have to drive the characters through a succinct set of quickly resolved problems, and it all needs to be wrapped up in 90≈minutes. Even if you're lucky enough to end up writing a sequel, you still have to solve the main conflicts of *this movie*. For that reason, your film has to pack a lot of action and character development into a very small time frame, so the scale can be — and often should be — massive.

Television, on the other hand, is usually produced on a much lower budget than film, so you have to take your time. Or, as I like to think of it, you *get* to take your time. It's a necessity in television that your stories, or "arcs," are stretched out over entire seasons and, hope-fully, over a series of seasons. It's not as simple as stretching out a film's plot over 13 to 25 episodes, of course, but it's an opportunity to explore what your characters will do in different situations and to watch them grow gradually and naturally. A TV series, whether realistic, fantastic, or surreal, is more like real life in that it takes time for big, sweeping changes to happen. Until the final episode of most seasons, of course, for which a lot of writers save massive events and changes, to keep everyone guessing what's going to happen next season.

Most comedy television is broken up into three or four acts that func-tion much the same way as a film's acts. However, they are often a bit more complex. While you're stretching out your character arcs (how your character develops over a period of time) over a season or sea-sons for that natural development, you have to make up for that lack of material density. Most sitcoms have an A story (primary plotline), a B story (secondary plotline) and, sometimes, a C story (minor plotline), which generally make appearances in all of your show's acts. Each story involves a basic conflict that is trying to be resolved. In a way, it's like three sketches, cut into three pieces, and spaced out. Often, these same stories will occur in the same space, at the same time, especially if your show takes place in mostly the same location (like a workplace comedy).

Your main concentration, as always, should be on your characters and what they're going through. A quick guide I always use is this: plot is what happens, and story is how your character deals with those things happening. Their development can only really be shown in how they deal with conflict, and that's true for all creative writing. When it comes to TV — especially comedy — you're often giving your main character and side characters multiple increasingly harrowing obstacles per episode to see how they all deal when the stakes are raised. At the end of the episode, sure, they tend to make it out unscathed, but we should want to know how they'll deal with whatever is thrown in their path next week.

The key to making characters fun to watch, which is the real point of even bothering to put them in these situations in the first place, is finding their weaknesses. Some people look at these as "personality quirks," but generally, you're trying to find the places where a character often deals poorly so we can watch them try extra hard just to get past those disruptions in their daily life or job. Here, you will find the comedy and/or drama in how they deal. For example, your main character might be obsessed with cleanliness. You can give this character relatively simple storylines, but if that storyline involves some level of filth to wade through, then it will be more fun to watch them deal with it. Of course, no matter how "simple" the storyline is, it needs to service where the character is going in the long run. Every time they conquer an obstacle, they should grow in some way.

Whenever you're writing a story, whether for TV or film, the key is determining whether or not you're writing something you'd like to watch. You can never start out thinking about what other people are going to want to see or read — you can tweak your idea to those specifications later. Your characters, their weaknesses, and the plots they're involved in, are all informed by your love of the world you've created. This is especially true for TV, when audiences will be "living" in this world for extended periods of time.

The audience, script readers, and potential producers will be able to tell if you care about what you're writing pretty much immediately. Passion alone can't sell a script or make it worth a read, but it is the first step. Step two is writing as much as you can, using your favorite TV shows as a loose template. Eventually, that passion combines with the writing skills you've gained simply by writing as often as possible, resulting in something you're not only passionate about, but something that somehow makes other people picture exactly what was in your head and allows them to realize that same world on the small screen.

Jason Klamm is the author of two books: Looking Forward: A Hopemoir (2008) and the fake internet history Post-Modem: The Interwebs Explained (2015). He is also the writer of the feature films Looking Forward and Lords of Soaptown. His works have found homes at NBC Universal, Comedy Central, and Frontier Airlines, and he has written films and TV pilots for Jamie Kennedy Entertainment. He is also the host of The Comedy on Vinyl Podcast, which shares a subject with his next book.

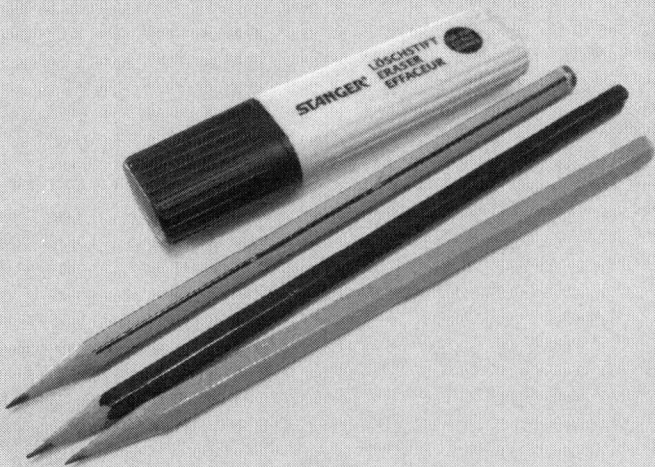

CHAPTER 2:

LEARNING FROM THE PROS

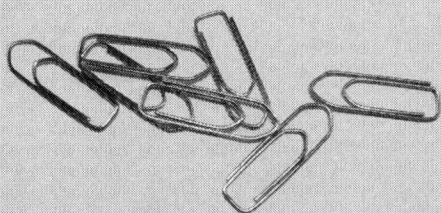

Writing a screenplay can be pretty intimidating if you've never actually seen a Hollywood script. How can you emulate something you're not familiar with? If you want to be a screenwriter, one of the first things you should do is read scripts. In this day and age, you can find them all over the internet.

Reading other scripts can give you a good sense of the world that's out there, and it'll help you set expectations for what it will take to break into the movie world.

Some sites have scripts divided by time period, with many different editions of each script. If you can find them, submission-stage scripts are the ones you'll want to look at, because at this stage, they aren't yet complicated with camera directions and technical things.

Try to read all kinds of scripts. Movies you love, movies you hate, movies from all kinds of genres. Read household names and unknown writers. The more you read, the better.

READING SCREENWRITING ONLINE

There are countless online resources available for you to find and read screenplays. Sites like The Internet Movie Script Database (**www.imsdb.com**), Simply Scripts (**www.simplyscripts.com**), and Drew's Script-O-Rama (**http://script-o-rama.com**) are useful ones to check out. Sites like these have many popular movies in script form that you can view or download.

Some of the biggest things you will learn from reading other scripts are formatting, style, and what exactly needs to be on the page. Though the format of a script is similar to a stage-play script, stage directions and camera directions should be left out, as the director and actors will collaborate on the movement and blocking of a scene. When trying to sell your script, readers are also going to gloss right over those parts anyway. Keep your screenplay basic with only essential story elements.

If you are used to writing fiction, it might take you a little time to adjust to the look of a script page. In screenwriting, there should be a lot of white space on the page. We'll focus on the specifics of formatting later in this book, but here's an example to give you a general idea.

```
INT-OFFICE-DAY


Sara and Mary stand at the copier. Sara
looks around to see if anyone is nearby
while Mary jabs randomly at the buttons.

                    MARY
          Do you think they know?


                    SARA
                    Who?


                    MARY
               All of them!


                    SARA
          How would they know?


                    MARY
     James saw us. On the security camera.
     It's only a matter of time before they
                   all know.
```

The copier begins to make a buzzing
noise. Both girls take a step back but
otherwise ignore it.

                    SARA
Why are you just now telling me this?

The copier beeps and starts spitting out
paper.

                    MARY
I just found out. I couldn't very well
come running right to your desk.

The average Hollywood script is about 100 pages long, and each page represents about one minute of screen time. Early in your career, writing a script longer than that is probably going to work against you when it comes to getting it sold. Readers will be looking for an excuse to put down your script, so don't give them a reason to before they even start.

Reading other scripts will also give you a good sense of pacing and when certain things typically happen. When you come across something you really enjoy, stop and think about what makes the scene work from a structural and storytelling perspective. Try to define what makes each scene necessary to the story. Think about what each character is hoping to achieve in each scene. All of these things will help when you sit down to write your own script.

Script reading checklist

Here are some things to look out for as you read through scripts:

- ➡ Who is the main character?

- ➡ What does he or she want to achieve?

- ➡ What will he or she do to achieve his or her goal?

- ➡ Who is trying to prevent the main character from getting what he or she wants?

- ➡ Why does this person want to stop the main character?

- ➡ What nonverbal clues does the writer give that hint at this person's personality?

- ➡ Is the love story convincing? Why or why not?

- ➡ What do you find charming about the love interest character?

- ➡ What clues does the screenwriter give you about the bad traits of a love interest?

- ➡ Are all of the things set up in the script paid off?

- ➡ Does the ending resolve all the plotlines?

- ➡ Was there ambiguity to the ending? Do you think this was intentional?

WATCHING AND ANALYZING MOVIES

Have you ever wanted to turn to your mom and yell, "I'm doing research!" while sitting on the couch watching a movie?

Well, now you can!

However, that doesn't mean you should take this lightly. Watching movies is an important part of research. You have to be devoting all of your attention to it, taking notes, and thinking constantly about why different storytelling decisions are being made in a film.

Watch movies in all kinds of genres — horror, suspense, comedy, family drama, etc. — to get a sense for the type of movies you prefer and those you don't care for. You can't figure out how you want to approach the craft until you get a good sense of how others do it.

Seeing how words are translated from the page to the screen should also help you as you think about your writing. It can be very useful to analyze the writing of a good scene to determine what made it work.

If you are struggling to analyze film, look for some kind of "Introduction to Film" class at an online or local community college. This can help you to understand the different roles involved in making a movie and to break down themes, story, and the elements that create a visual impact on the viewer.

ASK THE EXPERT: "Criticism, far from
sapping the vitality of art, is instead
what supplies its lifeblood… not an enemy
from which art must be defended, but rather
another name — the proper name — for the
defense of art itself."
 — A.O. Scott, film critic for the New York Times

Thinking about movies you like

When you come across movies that you like, you should take a closer look at them and think about what made them work for you. Here are some possible different factors.

The look and feel

Movies can be a place of comfort. They can make us feel at home and help us escape from our everyday struggles and fears. Movies can also make us deeply uncomfortable. They can give us visceral thrills and ask us questions we never wanted to ask ourselves.

Through writing, directing, set design, and other tricks, movies can evoke all kinds of feelings from the audience.

For example, movies like *Home Alone* (1990), which take place in northerly, wintery, snowy places, are designed to evoke feelings of Christmastime, family, and joy. A movie like *Twilight* (2008), a teenage romance story, takes place in Forks, Washington, the real-life rainiest place in America. The constant rainfall and blue overtones give the movie a creepy atmosphere. *Mamma Mia* (2008) puts the upbeat songs of Abba in the setting of a beautiful Grecian island to make the audience feel as if they have gone on a carefree vacation.

The communication style

Just like people themselves, movies have all different kinds of communication styles.

Some people prefer slick, fast-talking movies in which the characters and dialogue move so quickly that you will still notice new things on your third or fourth viewing (like a Shane Black or Quentin Tarantino movie). Others may prefer a slower pace, where each character takes time to evolve and speak his or her heart (like a Nicholas Sparks movie). One of the latest trends has been a genre of film known as "mumblecore," where a low-budget film is characterized by its use of naturalistic or improvised performances.

The opening

There are a countless number of ways that you can start a movie.

Pulp Fiction (1994) starts with a seemingly normal couple talking in a diner. Within minutes, they're robbing the place. This establishes the disjointed, frantic pace that the rest of the movie moves at. Some movies, like *Avengers: Age of Ultron* (2015), begin "in media res," or in the middle of things. In these instances, the viewer is dropped into some kind of climactic fight scene or shouting match that the movie then tends to work backwards from. Other movies open with a typical day in the characters' lives so that we can see how much they change during the movie, like *Thelma and Louise* (1991).

The style of humor

Many different styles of humor might appeal to you as a viewer. Movies like *American Pie* (1999) or *Knocked Up* (2007) have a raunchier style of humor that utilizes taboo subjects or disgusting situations to evoke laughter. Romantic comedies will often have a clumsy but cute heroine who provides the film with humor by embarrassing herself in adorable ways. Other movies, like *Marvel's* recent run of superhero films (2008-present), take a witty and sarcastic approach to humor.

Thinking about movies you hate

There are few things as frustrating as spending money on a movie that turns out to be really bad. However, a poor moviegoing experience can also help you to avoid the same mistakes as a screenwriter. Let's look at some of the common problems that occur in uneven films.

The same old story

Are you sick and tired of action and superhero movies because they all seem the same to you? Maybe you dislike romantic comedies because you find them to be too predictable. Perhaps you can't watch scary movies because you constantly find yourself baffled by the stupidity of the characters.

Movies are plagued by the tendency to tell stories that you've seen before. In your writing, you can try to use these "same old stories" to come up with innovative spins on typical storytelling techniques. Movies require structure, but that doesn't mean you can't play around and make a movie more interesting. Remember, your characters need to accomplish (or be trying to accomplish) something in each scene, but it doesn't have to be in the same way as every other movie.

Phony talk

A screenwriter's presence in a film can often feel like that of a sports official or referee. If you don't notice them or their work, then they're doing a good job. But if you do, it's bad news. Poor dialogue can rip an audience right out of a movie.

Don't put too much pressure on yourself, though. Even critically acclaimed filmmakers can struggle with writing good dialogue. For example, George Lucas — creator of *Star Wars* — has been frequently criticized for not writing very convincing dialogue. In *Episode II: Attack of the Clones* (2002), Padme and Anakin have the following conversation:

PADME
We used to come here for school retreat. We would swim to that island every day. I love the water. We used to lie out on the sand and let the sun dry us and try to guess the names of the birds singing.

ANAKIN
I don't like sand. It's coarse and rough and irritating, and it gets everywhere. Not like here. Here everything is soft and smooth.

Many common mistakes can render dialogue unconvincing and make it fall flat on the page. We'll cover tips and exercises for writing convincing dialogue later in this book in Chapters 3 and 4.

Controversial, ambiguous endings

Ambiguous, or open-ended, endings are not necessarily a bad thing. It can be artistically thrilling to end a movie ambiguously and can keep people talking about your movie for years. However, ambiguous endings can be quite polarizing among viewers. Many people may be frustrated to walk out of a movie theater feeling like nothing was resolved.

Take HBO's popular television series, *The Sopranos* (1999—2007). People were angry after its ambiguous series finale, as the screen cut to black with its main character sitting in a (possibly precarious) diner. Many fans and media were enraged by the lack of a clear ending, which series creator David Chase later said was the plan all along.

Movies like *Inception* (2010) and *Pulp Fiction* have also led to hundreds of thousands of words of internet debate thanks to ambiguities in their storytelling. As a screenwriter, whether you like open-ended endings or not, you have to be able to study and appreciate the merits of ending your story with varying degrees of closure.

Deus ex machina

"Deus ex machina" is a Greek term that roughly translates to "god out of the machine." In the tradition of Greek storytelling, an actual god would appear onstage and set everything right just when it seemed there was no way out. In practice, "deus ex machina" is a storytelling shortcut in which the solution to a complicated story drops out of the sky and magically pleases everyone.

You will find that this is used frequently in cinematic storytelling. Like ambiguous endings, this technique is not always bad but can be frustrating. Endings are hard to do; make sure yours is thought-out and considered in every way.

Tropes and original stories

Over the years, many clichés and narrative conventions have become an integral part of filmmaking and storytelling. Many of these storytelling devices can be referred to as tropes, or shortcuts for describing situations that the storyteller can reasonably assume the audience will recognize. Using familiar patterns and techniques can keep the story moving faster.

The site TV Tropes, found at **http://tvtropes.org,** can give you a good look at some examples of tropes in television and other media that fans have catalogued over the years, including common characters (Con Man, Hired Gun, Hero) and common dialogue tricks (exposition, informed conversation, one-liners).

FUN_FACT: One example of a common trope is the "Lazy Husband." This character is typically a husband who is only seen lounging around the house while his wife does all the work. She often berates him for being lazy. What other tropes have you noticed in entertainment?

Many people become frustrated by tropes, because they seem to stifle creativity in storytelling, but tropes are not inherently a bad thing. Deciding how you utilize them or undermine them is what really matters.

Many movies use common storytelling tropes to their advantage. For example, *The Princess Bride* (1987) uses its fairytale setting to take countless sly swipes at classic fairytale storytelling devices.

In the 2000s, there was a whole line of movies devoted to making fun of movies, including *Scary Movie* (2006), *Not Another Teen Movie* (2001), and *Epic Movie* (2007). *Scary Movie* took aim at the horror genre, which is loaded with tropes. For example, the girls in the movie run up the stairs to get away from the bad guys, and the villain refuses to die, surviving to come back and lunge at the hero one, two, or many more times.

Easter eggs

Writers often insert hidden messages or winks throughout their movies known as Easter eggs. For example, every Disney movie has many hidden Mickeys throughout. Whether it's the three-circle ears and head or the classic profile of Mickey's ears and nose in silhouette or a full-body Mickey, they are everywhere.

Knowing that should keep you entertained when your little brother or sister is watching *Finding Nemo* (2003) for the 4,000[th] time.

Here are some examples:

- While Lightning McQueen is re-paving the street before he can leave Radiator Springs in *Cars* (2006), one of the shops in the background has signs that make up a three-circle Mickey head.
- There's a Mickey in the sky as Mufasa gives Simba the speech on what it means to be a king during *The Lion King* (1994).
- As Mr. Incredible lands on the island in *The Incredibles* (2004), there's a hidden Mickey in the trees.

Keep an eye out!

The best American film of all time? Critics and moviegoers alike have frequently named Orson Welles' epic *Citizen Kane* (1941) as the best film ever made. Welles co-wrote and starred as Charles Foster Kane, a reclusive millionaire searching for his lost childhood. The movie is considered revolutionary because of the way its structure defied Hollywood conventions at the time, jumping around in flashbacks and using many different points of view.

Modern fans look to newer blockbusters that have changed the movie industry, like Steven Spielberg's *Jaws* (1975) or George Lucas' *Star Wars* (1977). There can be no true "best movie of all-time" due to the evolving and subjective nature of film, but these movies and others — *Vertigo* (1958), *2001: A Space Odyssey* (1968), *Casablanca* (1942), *Gone with the Wind* (1939) — have certainly made a large mark on the movie industry.

WATCHING FOREIGN FILMS

American directors and screenwriters aren't everything. Looking at what writers and directors from around the world are doing can help you a lot when making your screenplay.

For example, *Moulin Rouge* (2001) draws inspiration from India's Bollywood-style musical numbers. The climax of the film even features a dancer with the head of an elephant, commonly associated with the Hindu god, Ganesh.

I know what you're thinking. It sounds boring and frustrating to have to watch a movie where you need to read subtitles in order to keep up with the action.

But you can learn a lot from foreign films, and frankly, you will be missing out on a lot of great movies if you have a fear of subtitles.

Needless to say, some foreign films have been landmarks that have changed cinema in many ways.

Let's take a look at some of the most important filmmaking movements around the world.

The French New Wave

The French New Wave is one of the most influential movements in film. In the 1950s and 60s, French filmmakers were basically fed up with the conventional structure and storylines of traditional French cinema. Led by François Truffaut, Jean-Luc Godard, and Jacques Demy, French filmmakers rebelled by being original. They began to reject traditional structure to tell more imaginative, personal stories.

Using simple techniques, ordinary locations, and a low budget, these films were designed to shock the viewer with unexpected camera work and disjointed editing. They were also deeply personal stories. A classic example is Truffaut's *The 400 Blows* (1959), the story of Antoine, a well-meaning boy in a family troubled by infidelity who is rejected by his parents. Truffaut has said that the story has roots in his own personal troubled adolescence.

Japanese cinema

Japan's long and rich cinema history is highlighted by the 1950s, considered to be the Golden Age of Japanese filmmaking. During this time, the highly influential film *Seven Samurai* (1954) was released. The story is about seven samurai hired by a village to protect its crops, and it details the struggles between two different classes of people in Japanese society back in the 1500s. The film influenced many early American westerns.

Modern Japanese cinema has had an effect in America as well. For example, in the early 2000s, Japanese horror films gained a cult following in America. *Ringu* (1998) was even remade into *The Ring* (2002), starring Naomi Watts.

The size and scope of Bollywood

India's cinema industry rivals Hollywood's in its size and cash-earning power. Bollywood movies are typically characterized by extravagant and extensively choreographed musical numbers, which may seem nonsensical and unnecessary to American viewers, but are crucial in India.

The songs from Bollywood movies are often released to the public before the movie itself. People will listen to the music and use that to determine whether they see the movie. The quality of the music basically determines how the movie does at the box office.

In modern-day Bollywood, the films feature exotic locales like Miami or France and tell complicated stories that span different genres, typically relating to love and marriage. Audiences have been conditioned to expect a little bit of everything and to go on a roller coaster ride of emotions.

Tradition usually has movies adhere to India's stricter family values. The hero and heroine are typically seen sharing a kiss and nothing more.

These films can come close to three-hour running times and are usually shown with an intermission. With people of Indian descent all around the world and Westerners who have grown to become big fans, Bollywood has a following pretty much everywhere.

ASK THE EXPERT: "I would love to work in a Bollywood film as there is so much drama and color in the films there."

  – Brad Pitt, actor and three-time Academy Award acting nominee

The advance of Nollywood

Over the last couple of decades, Nigerian cinema has become much more popular and prolific. Nigeria currently produces the second-most films in any given year, more than even the United States (India is first).

Films are typically produced quickly and cheaply, without any of the luxuries of a Hollywood film. Rather than going directly into theaters, movies are then distributed on video or disc. But the movie industry has helped the Nigerian economy greatly, employing a large number of people and bringing in more money to the country.

Where to find classic and foreign films

Video stores are almost obsolete. You may even be reading this and thinking, "what the heck is a video store?" All you need to know is that without them, it has become a bit more work to find movies outside of mainstream new releases. Here are a couple of places to start.

➡ Online: The Criterion Collection streams online via Hulu Plus as part of a monthly subscription fee. Movies include *Seven Samurai, The 400 Blows, Harlan County USA,* and much more. Netflix also offers some classic movies through its streaming and DVD services.

➡ Specialty Channels: Turner Classic Movies frequently shows films from the 1930s with limited commercial interruption, uncut from their original form. IFC and the Sundance Channel often show acclaimed foreign films.

Now you've got an idea of what to look for and how to look out for it. Now, let's start preparing your script!

CASE STUDY: FIVE THINGS I WISH I KNEW FROM DAY ONE

Joel Dameron
Writer, Director, and Filmmaker
Twitter: @Electric_Candy_

In the true pursuit of any craft, you're continuously learning new techniques and honing your skills. There are, however, a few basics that I wish someone would have told me about when I first started.

Finding your voice

Think about the way you talk to your best friends. Now, think about the way you talk to the boy or girl you're dating. Now your parents, your teachers, your principal. Is each one a different voice? It probably is, and that's alright.

We all have different voices we take on in order to communicate with each other. It's natural. In writing, you want to find your truest voice, the one you use with those you're closest to. Start with that voice as the protagonist or antagonist of your story. Then, ask yourself a few questions. What is that person/animal/robot/whatever doing? Where are they? Why are they there? Who are they there with? Before you know it, you're writing a story.

Dialogue

Writing believable, non-robotic dialogue is important. Paying attention to people when they're talking to you can help. Although, sometimes it's just easier to watch how other people interact. It sounds weird, but it's actually what all writers do. You don't have to be a weirdo about it and stare at them, just quietly listen and observe. Then, you take the traits and/or characteristics that you find interesting in them and use them as a base for your characters. After a while, you'll have a pretty decent roster of characters.

I did this with my most recent screenplay, *BLUFF*. I used people I met while staying at a hotel. They were professional poker dealers who toured around the world to deal at the big poker tournaments.

You could also use your friends for characters. I did that with a script I wrote a couple of years ago called *HITTERS*, which became my feature film debut. A good rule of thumb is to try to write how you naturally speak.

Eventually, you'll run out of characters, and you'll actually have to go places and do things and experience life. Those experiences will change you, sometimes negatively, and you'll learn things about the world and yourself. These are the things that make the best stories.

Remember, there is no art without pain. Sometimes you have to let yourself take it all in, think about how it made you feel and decide what it meant, if it meant anything.

Lastly, have you heard the famous saying "write what you know"? Well, that's crap. Don't write what you *know*. Write what you *don't know* but would like to know and by the end of the script, you'll probably be an expert on it.

Watch films

You can't write a film if you don't know what one looks like. I know it sounds simple, but what I mean is you have to watch as many films as possible. Then, watch them again, and again, and then watch how the story is structured and how each scene is laid out. Watch every kind of film, even those in genres you hate, because a writer who can write in any style is a writer who can always get paid. I have an 80/20 rule. This means 80 percent of the time, I watch amazing films with amazing scripts and learn what *to* do. The other 20 percent of the time, I watch bad movies with terrible scripts and learn what *not* to do.

NOTE: The definition of "bad" and "good" should probably be those that are collectively agreed upon as bad or good by film critics rather than your own personal preference.

Read

It's always good to physically see how others do it. So, find your favorite scripts and read them. You can usually find a copy online.

Have no fear

Don't be afraid to write badly. When you do, toss it and keep going. Failure is inevitable. You will fail, but just remember that your greatest success usually comes on the heels of your greatest failure.

The best writing advice I ever heard was from a famous screenwriter — I don't remember who — but basically what he said was, "Always have something to say." A writer who always has something to say is a writer that will never stop writing.

Joel Dameron is a Native American filmmaker, writer, musician, and photographer. Since 2011, he's written and directed over a dozen short films and music videos. His feature film debut, HITTERS, has been set for a 2016 release. He just finished writing his next feature, BLUFF, which has been slated for 2017. He currently resides in southeastern Oklahoma, where he lives with his wife, Brooke.

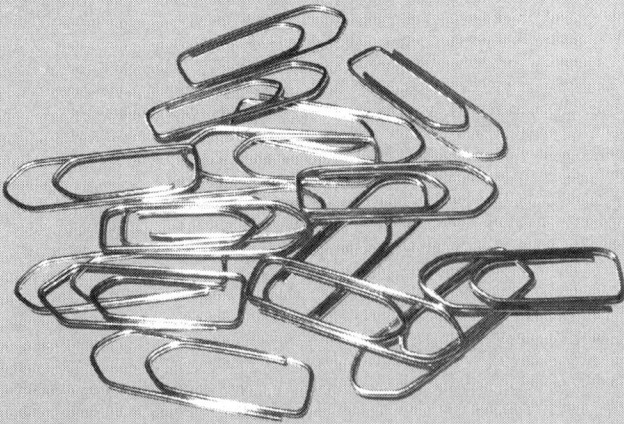

CHAPTER 3:

GETTING STARTED: FOCUSING ON YOUR STORY

Now that you've seen some of the work that other filmmakers and screenwriters have done, it's time to focus on your script. In this chapter, we'll cover doing research for your idea, setting your idea apart, creating characters, and writing scenes.

RESEARCH

Once you have an idea for a screenplay, you need to research. No matter your idea — fictional or nonfictional, taking place on Earth or on an alien planet — you absolutely have to research. Prepare yourself for an audience that might try to tear your movie apart.

Location

Setting is crucial. You have to learn about the actual location of your story. Study maps, and read up on its history. Maybe you'll want to visit places to truly capture the mentality of those who live there. The animators and writers of *Cars*, for instance, drove along historic Route 66 to study all of the small towns along the way.

Your setting can function as an important character in your movie, so make sure it is strongly considered and well thought-out before you start writing.

Language

People in particular areas of the country and world can have very distinctive dialects. Slang words and colloquialisms might be more popular in some areas than others. Different words might be considered vulgar in different countries.

The way your characters talk in your script can be crucial to revealing things about them or the setting.

In *Mean Girls* (2004), Gretchen Wieners, one of the popular girls, repeatedly uses the word "fetch" to refer to something cool. No matter how hard she tries, though, the word never catches on. Eventually, the queen Mean Girl, Regina George, tells Gretchen to stop trying so hard to make "fetch" cool. In the overall story, it serves as a development in their friendship's impending end, and it's all built out of one word.

Language is also important in establishing the authenticity of your film.

In *Hustle and Flow* (2005), use of the right slang gives the film authenticity and strengthens its sense of place. If DJ, the central character, spoke in perfect English, the story would not be as believable.

Occupation

Being familiar with the jobs of your main characters is crucial to making your movie feel realistic and authentic. If a construction worker is watching your construction worker character and thinking, "No construction worker would ever do that," this can take him or her completely out of the movie. Make sure you know the ins and outs of your characters' occupations so that any change you make will be intentional and serve your story.

This also applies to children, believe it or not. Even those who do not necessarily collect a paycheck still have a job within the family and a potentially important role to play in your script. Think about what kinds of hobbies and activities occupy the time of your friends and younger siblings when writing younger characters.

Time period

Movies that take place in a time older than our own, also known as period films or period pieces, require much more research than present-day films. Screwing up details of a period piece can subject you to harsh criticism and backlash. If something is shown to be patently untrue, it will turn off a lot of viewers. The defense that something is a work of fiction and not meant to be historically accurate will probably not stand up.

The movie *10,000 BC* (2008) was heavily criticized for its lack of resemblance to the historical time period. The story concerned D'Leh, a tribesman who crosses the treacherous ancient world to re-capture his love, Evolet. Here are some of the chief criticisms that were aimed at the film:

➡ The main actors spoke in English, a language that certainly didn't exist in 10,000 BC.

➡ Animals that looked like dinosaurs appeared in the film. Dinosaurs were definitely extinct by 10,000 BC.

➡ The people in the society that D'Leh finds worship a leader known as the Almighty. However, during that historical period, people were more likely to worship a sun god than a human on Earth.

➡ Weapons that were not created until much later were used in the film's battles.

➡ Animals were portrayed as being under the control of humans, which did not occur until later in history. In 10,000 BC, man was still using inanimate objects to help with tasks, like using gourds to carry water.

Roland Emmerich, the film's director, has defended his film's "creative freedom" since its release. He said he wanted the movie to be a representation of a lost society. He chose to make the movie in English so the audience could get emotionally involved.

As an established director, Emmerich had the leeway to make creative decisions like this. For first-time screenwriters, the same courtesy and freedom is generally not extended. A reader who goes over a script from a first-time writer that does not seem accurate will most likely toss it aside.

Research tools

Alright, so I need to research. How do I go about it? Here are a few tried and true ways to research a topic.

Books

Look hard enough, and you can find books on pretty much any topic. Keep in mind that research via books can be expensive if you are running to a local bookstore and buying each one. Keep research costs low by picking up books at the library, flea market, secondhand shop, yard sales, or discount websites (such as **www.half.ebay.com**).

Interviews

Make phone calls. Knock on doors. Stop people in the street. The only thing stopping you from getting great, personal anecdotes is your own nervousness and shyness.

Find subjects online (LinkedIn groups are a great option) and through friends. Ask people you know if they know anyone with knowledge about the subject you're researching. Call the public relations office of your local community college or university, and see if they can recommend a professor with some knowledge of your topic whom you can interview. Most of the time, you'll find that people will be happy to answer your questions.

Be courteous in your interviews. Arrive on time, and be prepared with your questions. Use a tape or digital recorder to help save you from scrambling to take notes.

Movies

There are probably other movies on the same topic that you are re-searching. Some writers feel that taking in other forms of media will negatively influence their creativity, but reading what already exists on a certain subject is the best way to avoid duplicating it.

Fact-finding trips

Scouting locations can be a high-cost endeavor, something that only established writers can afford to do. However, you might be able to find something local that will assist you in your work. For example, if you want to craft a period piece set in Spain, but you can't afford to fly to Spain, look for Spanish influences in America. There are many instances of Spanish architecture in states like Florida, California,

and even Minnesota, where there is a house created in the style of the famous Alhambra palace in Spain.

After you've done your research, you should re-examine your original story idea. Will it work in the given historical restraints? If your main character is a doctor, does it make sense for him to offer unsolicited advice to homeless people on the subway if this opens him up to legal liability? Can you write a movie that feels like it takes place in Pamplona? Make sure your story can fit with the research that you've come up with.

GENRE

As you focus your story and make your idea more and more specific, your story will hopefully become something distinctive that stands on its own. From a marketing standpoint, though, studios will be looking for a way to categorize your movie so that they can sell it to audiences.

Take a movie like *The Blind Side* (2009). The journey of Michael Oher — who starts the movie sleeping on the streets and ends up being drafted to the National Football League — is a moving drama, a feel-good family story, a comedy, and a sports movie. Studios might choose to simply market it as a moving drama, though. Categorizing a movie helps the audience know what to expect from the experience and leaves more to be discovered when they actually see it.

Here are some common genres that define film:

➡ **Action** — These movies often center on big action set pieces, fighting, or martial arts. *Die Hard* (1988), *The Transporter* (2002), and Jackie Chan movies are all good examples.

- **Comedy** — Movies designed to make us laugh, even if they are telling a heartfelt story at the same time. Examples in this genre spread far and wide, but include films like *Knocked Up*, *Bad Teacher* (2011), *Airplane!* (1980), *Anchorman* (2004), and *Dumb and Dumber* (1994).
- **Drama** — Emotional stories that take the viewer on a journey. There are far too many examples to include, but *The King's Speech* (2010), *Titanic* (1997), *Cast Away* (2000), and *There Will Be Blood* (2007) are all thought of as dramas.
- **Family** — Movies that the whole family can enjoy together. Can include family comedies like *Freaky Friday* (2003), animated features like *Finding Nemo* or *The Lion King*, or live-action movies like *Spy Kids* (2001) and *The Sisterhood of the Traveling Pants* (2005).
- **Horror** — Movies designed to scare and delight, whether through suspense or gore. Examples include *Paranormal Activity* (2007), *The Hills Have Eyes* (2006), and *The Shining* (1980).
- **Romance** — Sentimental stories like *When Harry Met Sally* (1989), *The Notebook* (2004), and *500 Days of Summer* (2009).
- **Biography** — Movies that tell the story of someone's life. These can include stories about famous entertainers [*Walk The Line* (2005)], historical figures [*Capote* (2005)], or regular people with extraordinary stories [*Erin Brockovich* (2000)].
- **Science fiction** — Modern-day creature features [*Cloverfield* (2008)], apocalypse movies [*2012* (2009)], and alien movies [*Independence Day* (1996)] all fall into this genre.
- **Superhero** — There is rarely a spot on the calendar when there isn't a superhero movie playing in a nearby theater. These include Marvel's *Avengers* movies, DC's Justice League films, and others, like *Chronicle* (2012) and the *X-Men* series.

FUN FACT: If you don't think superhero movies deserve their own genre, check the box office. Without adjusting for inflation, movies starring superheroes take up four of the top 10 slots among the highest grossing U.S. movies of all-time. (Stats according to BoxOfficeMojo.com.)

SETTING YOUR IDEA APART

In Hollywood, everything old is constantly being made new again. Remakes and reboots litter the box office. Look at 2015. *Mad Max: Fury Road, Jurassic World, Terminator Genisys, Pan, Poltergeist, Point Break, Fantastic Four,* and *Star Wars Episode VII: The Force Awakens* were all movies based off previously existing ideas or franchises.

Sometimes it can seem like the same idea is just being passed around, like when *No Strings Attached* and *Friends with Benefits* came out within weeks of each other in 2011 or *White House Down* and *Olympus Has Fallen* came out within months of each other in 2013.

It can be easy for a young screenwriter to think that Hollywood doesn't want new, original ideas. Movie executives want to make money, first and foremost. Any idea with a built-in audience — like reboots and remakes — is an easier sell than something new and outside the box. This can be frustrating, but nostalgia is a powerful selling point. Some movies don't even have to be good to make money, because all that matters is the presence of a certain character or actor.

It is also risky for studios to spend money on a property no one has ever heard of when they can go with something people know and love. If you like *Wall Street* (1987), you can expect *Wall Street:*

Money Never Sleeps (2010) to satisfy your desires and follow a similar path to the first film. Man enters stock market, man learns greed is good, man gets in way over his head, and so on and so forth. The details will have changed just enough to keep you interested but stayed similar enough to keep you comfortable.

So what should your approach be as a screenwriter?

Don't let Hollywood standards irritate you. Use them to your advantage. Find a trope or genre that your idea may be similar to, and infuse it with a new energy or fresh perspective. Write your characters so that they don't fit into whatever archetype came before. Give your characters distinctive traits to make them memorable. For example, one of the main characters in HBO's television series *The Leftovers* likes to relieve stress by putting on a bulletproof vest and having people shoot her in the chest.

Perhaps the way that you write will add flavor to your script. *Juno* (2007) told a typical story of an unexpected pregnancy, but it became more sweet, comedic, and memorable by keeping true to the language of the modern teenager.

Find ways to add idiosyncratic, personal touches to your screenplay to make it truly yours.

CREATING CHARACTERS

The best way to make your movie stand out is by creating memorable characters. Coincidentally, if you are having trouble focusing and developing your story, getting to know your characters is the first thing you should do. Thinking about the backgrounds and worldviews of your characters will help shape the story and determine how they would deal with different conflicts that arise.

For example, let's say you have an average person — an Alaskan fisherman who marries a Hollywood celebrity. He might not fit in with her Hollywood friends. She doesn't fit in with his hard-working, conservative family. You have to dig deeper and make this idea more specific.

Let's say that your fisherman proposes marriage. To inform your Hollywood starlet's decision, think about her history and background. Maybe she fled from a conservative upbringing to follow her dreams. Perhaps she has always wanted to go home again to see her parents but has never had the nerve. With the Alaskan fisherman as her husband, she might have hope of reuniting with them.

Next, think of the fisherman. If they do get married, maybe he doesn't know how to deal with living in Hollywood. He might be uncomfortable in a big mansion and unsure of how to spend his days. Maybe his father was an alcoholic who drank himself to death, and he is terrified that his loneliness in L.A. might lead to a similar end.

You'll find that your characters' backgrounds can help dictate and expand story ideas to keep your screenplay moving and full of energy. Take the time to get to know your characters and what they want. This will help make your story the best it can be.

FUN FACT: Harrison Ford's Indiana Jones character is one of the most famous movie characters of all time. The character, created by George Lucas, was originally named Indiana Smith before Steven Spielberg requested a change.

Creating believable characters

It's just as important for your characters to be believable. With rare exception, the audience will need something resembling humanity out of your characters in order to come along for the ride. The way you reveal the full depth of your characters also has to be believable. Doing this through dialogue can be very difficult. Think about whether what you are writing is something a person would say.

For example, no one talks like this:

> JAKE
> You know, Mike, you're my best friend. Ever since I got home from Iraq, where I spent four hard years, me and my wife just haven't been the same.

Here's a better way to say the above without coming right out and saying it:

> MIKE
> How have things been since you got home?
>
> JAKE
> Good, I suppose. Glad to see my kids. Damn happy my Harley's still running after four years in the garage.
>
> MIKE
> What about Laura?
>
> JAKE
> Laura doesn't say much.

The words of your characters are important, but *how* they say things is almost as important. Think about what the audience might assume about your characters because of what they *aren't* saying. In the above scene, Mike should come across as a concerned friend, because he is asking questions about Jake's life that imply he cares about what's going on with him.

Characters you need

The protagonist

Every movie will have at least one protagonist, the person the story is about. The screenplay will typically follow this person's journey to get what he or she wants. The audience has to be intrigued or compelled by this character in some way so that they are invested in where the story is going. This doesn't mean the character has to be likable, but they need to be relatable or recognizably human in some way. The movie will detail this character's journey and transformation as he or she tries to achieve his or her goals.

The likability factor

An unlikable person can be at the center of a likable movie. Typically, he or she will have to become slightly more tolerable as the film progresses. At the very least, the audience needs to have some reason to be interested in following along. Author Blake Snyder (*Save The Cat!*) advises screenwriters to take a moment early in the screenplay to make the character likable or redeemable in some way.

The reluctant protagonist

A reluctant protagonist can still potentially be a protagonist. Some screenwriting scholars have argued that Cameron, Ferris Bueller's best friend in *Ferris Bueller's Day Off* (1986), is the true protagonist of the story. As the movie progresses, Ferris doesn't have much of an arc or change at all, but Cameron changes a lot and learns to stand up to his overbearing father. You could make an argument that the movie is actually "about" him.

The antagonist

The antagonist is the character whose goals clash most strongly with the protagonist's. He or she might be explicitly trying to stop the protagonist, or he or she might just desire a different outcome than the protagonist does.

For example, your protagonist might be hoping for a big promotion at work. If your antagonist is trying to stop him or her at any cost, he or she would act differently than an honest, hardworking antagonist who simply hopes to win the same promotion.

The obstacles that stand in between your hero and his or her goals will make your movie compelling. Many of these obstacles will come from your antagonist's attempts to stop the protagonist. Think of The Joker in *The Dark Knight* (2008) or Loki in *The Avengers* (2012). They are antagonists constantly putting up obstacles to stop the protagonists of their movies.

The antagonist should usually have recognizable and understandable motivations. Without them, an evil, mean-spirited antagonist can be really difficult to pull off. In *Cars*, Lightning McQueen's nemesis, Chick Hicks, fights dirty. Over the course of the film, we learn that Chick has been a perpetual runner-up his whole life and is fighting dirty because he is simply tired of losing.

The reflection

The reflection character is essentially the voice of reason in your film. This character is the best friend, the person the protagonist can turn to in a bind, the person he or she can spill his or her deepest secrets to. This character can help the protagonist devise a course of action or help enact whatever plan the protagonist has. The reflection can also serve as the voice of the audience and air the skepticisms that they might have.

In *My Best Friend's Wedding* (1997), Rupert Everett calmly asks Julia Roberts who else is chasing her as she chases the groom. She says no one, and he points this out. Even though she doesn't listen to him, this shows the audience that not everyone in the film's universe is stupid and unrealistic.

The romance character

Your movie does not need a love story to be successful, but having one is a common trope in movies. Who isn't a sucker for a good romance? A love interest can propel your protagonist's story or highlight their shortcomings and goals. Often, the protagonist thinks that capturing his or her love interest will result in a better life. The protagonist might have to become a better person to attract the love interest. Romance can be a powerful story driver.

ASK THE EXPERT: "The key to creating better plot rests in a deeper understanding of character."

— Kristen Lamb, author of "Rise of the Machines — Human Authors in a Digital World"

CASE STUDY:
CRAFTING YOUR CHARACTERS

Loretta Lang
Writer and Director
www.jlightfilm2talent.com

When writing a screenplay, you will probably rethink and edit the scenes and dialogue more times than you can count. The most important thing is establishing your main and supporting characters early on and finding a proper balance between them. Don't make the supporting character's life more interesting than the main character's. This will leave the audience wanting things out of your film that they won't get. Knowing your characters and their roles is extremely important!

Main Character
Your main character is the person the story is about. In most cases, it's usually one person or thing (if you want to have animals that can talk or something). It takes a master screenwriter to write more than one main character. In order to develop this character, his or her state at the beginning of the movie should be different than the end, meaning that if Dan has an anger management problem at the beginning, he should be "sweet as pie" at the end or should become the leader of an anger management group. That's character development. See what I mean?

So, how do you actually develop the main character during the screenplay? First, consider the character's reality. Where does he live, work, and eat? How does she walk and talk? Does he have an accent? Is she from a rich home, or she live in poverty? Why is he angry? Is your character angry with his family or society? You have to know everything about this character at all times to be able to track and show the change at the end.

Think about how the main character relates to others, such as his or her mother, siblings, co-workers, and neighbors. All of these things are important. When the character is placed in a certain situation, will you see certain behaviors? The character's response to internal and external factors — as determined by you, the writer — should be natural human responses and not fabricated ones. For example, if the character gets nervous around a certain group of people, the character's dialogue and action should reflect it. Basically, his dialogue can't be, "I love you guys so much," while his facial expression suggests confusion (as noted in the action line).

Characterization

Treat your characters as everyday people. You don't have to go far to find a loser, an introvert, a complainer, or an agitator. They're all around. Try to study people so that you can understand the ways that certain people react to different situations. A courageous fireman would not bite his fingernails when he hears a fire alarm. However, if an old lady is in a similar situation, she would probably panic. As a screenwriter, you have to be thinking about the way real people would act when determining the dialogue and action of the character.

Have fun creating your character. He or she can be "over-the-top" or reserved and bashful. Try to make the character distinctive and unpredictable. If you're not having fun, who's going to have fun watching your work?

Loretta Lang is the owner of JLight Film and Talent Productions, a full-service production company dedicated to the creation of faith-based film projects. She is the screenwriter and director of "The Good Fight of Faith" film — to be released in 2017.

WRITING SCENES

You can think about your characters and big-picture story all you want, but eventually, you're going to have to sit down and write scenes. When structuring scenes, you should think of each one as its own mini-movie. A scene should have its own conflicts and its own energy, separate from the story as a whole. Each scene needs to be long enough to convey its important points, but not so long that the audience is begging for it to end.

Remember, each script page translates to roughly one minute of screen time. There are no set rules as to how long a scene should be, but generally, they will last anywhere from a fraction of a page to up to a few pages. Scenes as long as five pages will probably be a rarity, and you shouldn't have more than a couple in your screenplay when you are still starting out.

Each scene needs to have something happen that moves the story forward. Even if the scene is just focusing on what is taking place in the characters' lives that day, the events of the scene need to have some long-term effect on the protagonist, the way he or she relates to other characters, or events that are going to take place later. Until you are an amazing writer, it's going to be really difficult to write scenes that don't move the story forward while also maintaining the story's energy and momentum. You don't want your audience members to turn to one another and say, "Well, what was the point of that?"

As you prepare to write a scene, start with the essentials. What are your characters doing? Where is the scene taking place?

For scenes that take place indoors, you will write "INT" for interior. For scenes that take place outdoors, you will write "EXT" for exterior.

When your story changes location, begin the new scene with a heading. For example, "EXT-LIGHTHOUSE-DAY" would mean you are outside in a lighthouse setting during the day. "INT-RESTAURANT-NIGHT" could place your characters in a Chinese restaurant at night.

Next, you will write what is happening in the scene. How can you describe it simply and succinctly on the page? This could look like this:

INT-RESTAURANT-NIGHT

Emma and Dave are at a Chinese restaurant, having dinner.

The next step is describing the setting a little bit. What does the reader need to know about the set-up or layout of this particular Chinese restaurant and Emma and Dave's position in it to understand the action? Try to convey this in a concise way that can be interpreted and represented visually.

INT—RESTAURANT—NIGHT

Emma and Dave are at a Chinese restaurant, having dinner. They have clearly been given the worst seat in the house, a small, uneven table right next to the kitchen doors.

Make sure you use simple words to describe the scene and action. Overwrought descriptions will slow the reader down. Try to be to the point and use words that would appear in just about anyone's vocabulary.

Remember to focus on visual descriptions and not character backstories. Everything you write should be able to be conveyed onscreen while leaving room for the director's interpretation.

For example, this character description is too specific for a screenplay.

Sarah, 45, Emma's mom, 10 years sober, is blonde with blue eyes. She carries the demons of her misspent youth with her, in the form of a limp.

Here's a better example:

Sarah, 45, is Emma's mom, and it is evident she was once beautiful like her daughter. She twirls an AA coin in her hand as she limps quickly along the sidewalk.

That's one way to write in a small character detail that can be extremely important down the road. Since the limp is just part of Sarah's gait, the viewer might draw the conclusion that this is an old injury. Later, you can reveal that she injured herself and Emma in a car accident, which led her to stop drinking.

Let's take a look at a fully fleshed-out example. This scene is about Emma, who is getting up early for work, and Sarah, who can't sleep.

```
INT-EMMA'S HOUSE-DAY

Emma walks into the kitchen in her work
uniform. Sarah is already at the table,
reading the Bible. The morning sun shines
through the blinds.

                    EMMA
              You're up early.

                   SARAH
        Couldn't sleep. What time are you working?

                    EMMA
          7:30. Elaine's picking me up.

                   SARAH
              Tell her I said hi.
```

> EMMA
> I will.
>
> Emma turns to leave, then looks back at Sarah.
>
> Maybe you should check out that meeting on Seventy-First and Fifth. They have good donuts at that coffee shop on the corner.
>
> SARAH
> Maybe I will.
>
> Emma puts on her uniform hat and walks out.

Think about how much is happening between the lines in this scene. Emma doesn't come right out and say what she means — "You're acting weird, and I'm concerned about your sobriety" — but she reminds her mom of the Alcoholics Anonymous meeting held nearby.

The viewer can see there is a conflict here. Emma wants her mom to stay sober, and Sarah is losing her will to do so. There are a lot of words left unsaid in the scene that will draw viewers in and pique their curiosity. Why can't Emma come out and say what she means? What is the history of Emma and Sarah's relationship and Sarah's struggle with sobriety? As the story goes on, the viewer will have more and more information revealed to them.

FUN FACT: The site RunPee (www.runpee.com) is a database of moments viewers have decided are "missable" in movies. The app tells you, with a visual timeline, which parts of the movie are not crucial and what you will miss if you run to the bathroom during the action. As you look over your own script, ask yourself, is this a scene where audience members will want to leave to use the bathroom?

Building energy in a scene

Action within scenes is important. Some writers like to start their scenes with a bang. The movie *Speed* (1994) opens with a scene where a SWAT team is rescuing a group of people in a booby-trapped elevator. The story drops the viewers right into the action while also setting things up — the use of bombs to trap and terrorize innocent people — that will come back during the story's main plotline. Scenes like this give the audience a jolt and hopefully put them on the edge of their seats.

Scenes can also start slow and build toward some kind of conflict. This creates tension and suspense if you are writing a thriller or horror film. Pacing the reveal of information in your story is key. Don't drag things out too long. Everyone's seen the scene where the hero is stalking slowly around the house, with the killer hidden somewhere. Paced well, it can create suspense and make the viewer squirm. Paced too slowly, the audience might lose their sense of fear and dismiss the entire movie. Maybe you can make the killer pop up very early in a scene like this to undercut the viewer's typical expectations.

Let's say you are working on a scene where a customer complains about Laura and the manager asks Emma to handle it. Emma is friends with Laura, so she knows this is a test to see if she is mature enough to act like a manager. The goal of this scene is to show Emma's progress in her job.

Originally, the scene opens like this:

INT-BAKERY COUNTER-DAY

Laura stands behind the bakery counter, looking across the rest of the store, as though she is waiting for someone to show up. She is wearing a full face of makeup and jewelry. A customer approaches the counter.

> CUSTOMER
> Hi. What kind of grains are in the whole bread?

> LAURA
> The grainy kind.

> CUSTOMER
> No, really.

> LAURA
> They're really grainy.

> CUSTOMER
> Did you wake up on the wrong side of the bed or something?

> LAURA
> Do you have some desire to never wake up again?

> CUSTOMER
> Did you just threaten me?

INT-BAKERY COUNTER-FIVE MINUTES LATER

Emma comes around the corner to find the manager standing next to Laura, who is yelling incoherently at the customer. The customer has picked up a baguette and is swinging it at Laura.

                         EMMA
                    What's going on?

The customer turns toward Emma, now swinging the
baguette wildly in all directions.

                        CUSTOMER
                   Don't come any closer!

                         EMMA
          Sir, just put the bread down, let's talk about
                          this.

                        CUSTOMER
                    (puts the bread down)

This woman threatened me! If she isn't fired, I'm
never shopping here again.

                        MANAGER
          Sir, I'm the manager here, and I'd be happy to
                    resolve this for you.

A voice calls the manager to customer service over
the intercom.

                        MANAGER
          I apologize, sir. I'm going to have to go take care
          of that. But Emma here is one of my best senior
          staff, and I trust her completely to take care of
                          this.

The manager walks away from the bakery counter. As
he passes Emma, he leans over and hisses in her ear.

                        MANAGER
                       Fix this!

As you re-write this scene, you might want to consider starting it when Emma shows up to speed up the pacing and give it more energy. This also gives you more time to deal with the resolution. The set-up here isn't completely necessary because even if you cut everything that occurs between Laura and the customer, the audience will be able to figure out what they missed. Laura was rude, the situation escalated, and now the customer wants her fired.

The ticking clock

Humanity as we know it is about to meet its end. The protagonist's true love is about to leave town forever. A wedding that the hero cannot miss is fast approaching. Adding a ticking clock, or time element, to your movie can increase tension.

Some famous films that feature a time element:

Ferris Bueller's Day Off: Ferris has to end his day of skipping school and be back in bed before his parents get home from work so that they will remain convinced that he is sick.

Beauty and The Beast (1991): In this Disney classic, the enchantment put on the beast centers on a magic rose. If the rose dies before the beautiful girl falls in love with him, he will be stuck in his beastly form forever.

Black Swan (2010): From the beginning of the movie, the audience is aware that the company is moving toward a production of *Black Swan*. Without being told, they can probably assume that the opening night of the ballet will conclude the film.

ASK THE EXPERT: "There is a distinct difference between "suspense" and "surprise," and yet many pictures continually confuse the two. I'll explain what I mean.

"We are now having a very innocent little chat. Let's suppose that there is a bomb underneath this table between us. Nothing happens, and then all of a sudden, 'Boom!' There is an explosion. The public is surprised, but prior to this surprise, it has seen an absolutely ordinary scene, of no special consequence. Now, let us take a suspense situation. The bomb is underneath the table and the public knows it, probably because they have seen the anarchist place it there. The public is aware the bomb is going to explode at one o'clock and there is a clock in the decor. The public can see that it is a quarter to one. In these conditions, the same innocuous conversation becomes fascinating because the public is participating in the scene. The audience is longing to warn the characters on the screen: 'You shouldn't be talking about such trivial matters. There is a bomb beneath you and it is about to explode!'

"In the first case we have given the public fifteen seconds of surprise at the moment of the explosion. In the second we have provided them with fifteen minutes of suspense. The conclusion is that whenever possible the public must be informed. Except when the surprise is a twist, that is, when the unexpected ending is, in itself, the highlight of the story." -Alfred Hitchcock, five-time Academy Award nominee and one of the most acclaimed directors of all-time

The business of the scene

Showing your characters' emotions rather than simply telling the audience what they are is important to an effective, emotionally honest film. As a young screenwriter, giving your character something to do in the scene other than just talking can make this much easier. Too many scenes featuring the characters simply talking to each other might be difficult to write and make your movie seem slow.

Use the fact that movies are a visual medium to your advantage. Let where your characters are and what they are doing tell the audience things about them.

Just to get your brain moving a little bit, here are some different things you might be able to have characters do:

➡ Change a tire or oil in a car instead of driving it
➡ Cook a meal together instead of just sitting at a restaurant
➡ Do one another's nails instead of going to a nail salon
➡ Go through their clothes and choose items to give to charity rather than shopping for new clothes
➡ Ride bicycles or walk instead of driving somewhere

Setting the tone of your scenes

Conveying the tone of your story is difficult as a screenwriter, given the limited amount of words you have to work with. The director, cinematographer, and set designers will also have a lot of influence over the final look of the movie. However, there are things you can do as a writer to set the tone.

The lighting and where you set a scene can do a lot to influence the mood. A daytime scene in a sunny yellow kitchen with lots of windows creates a happy, cheerful mood. A darker room sets a gloomier tone. You can also place items of a certain color in the scene to convey mood. The weather in your scene can greatly affect things as well.

The activities your characters are doing will also have a certain effect. If your characters are having fun, the audience will, too. Make sure the tone of your movie feels honest and consistent throughout. And remember, you have to convey these things using only brief scene descriptions and dialogue.

Putting the cherry on top

The last thing you need to do is simple. Make the audience want to watch the next scene. And the next scene. And the one after that. Putting a cherry on top — or writing a "button" — can help your scene leave a lasting impression as the audience moves on to the next one. Here's an example:

```
INT-KITCHEN-DAY


Wife is putting freshly baked cookies
on a cooling rack. Husband comes in and
tries to steal one.


                    WIFE
No, these are for my bake sale. Go away!

                 HUSBAND
          Come on, just one.
```

WIFE

No. I said no! Get out!

Husband leaves. Wife finishes with cookies and walks away. Husband runs back in and reaches out to steal one.

WIFE
(off screen)

I said no!

Husband slumps away.

The button should give a definite ending point, perhaps add a little levity to the scene, and provide a fresh, new energy for the audience to take into the next scene. A good one can make the audience feel ready for the next scene but also feel like the previous one ended on a high note.

One example is from *Pretty Woman* (1990). There's a scene where Julia Roberts goes back to the Rodeo Drive boutique she was chased out of the day before so that she can tell off the saleslady. She blows right by a saleslady who offers her help, shopping bags in hand, so that she can go confront the saleslady from the day before. As she's walking away, she says, "Big mistake. Big. Huge. I have to go shopping now."

There is nothing left for either character to say. And the audience is ready for whatever comes next.

Surprising the viewer with what they already know

No matter how hard you try to keep your movie fresh and original, parts of the movie will seem obvious to some viewers. If you have two lovers keeping secrets from one another, those secrets are probably going to come out. If there's a villain and a hero, they will probably face off at some point, and the hero will win.

You do not want anything in your story to feel inevitable, though. You want your audience to be so swept up in the moment that they will forget they had it all figured out. Keep the story moving. Don't give the audience time to think about where it's all headed. Work in subplots to keep their minds occupied. But do not play dumb. Assume your audience is as smart as you are.

You also have to remember that the audience knows more than your characters do most of the time. That's just the way movies work. But if you can keep the audience invested and excited, they might forget what they already know so that they can be surprised.

But there's a lot more to storytelling than just surprise. Let's zoom out a little bit and get into some storytelling tips.

ACT 1
*at the
dinner*

ACT 2
road trip

ACT 3
*the
wedding*

CHAPTER 4:

STORYTELLING 101

THE END

Alright, try not to get intimidated. We've talked about what makes a good screenwriter. We've talked about studying other movies, creating characters, writing scenes, and honing in on your idea. Now it's time to make sure it all holds together. It's time to focus on the big picture. How is your entire screenplay going to play out? This part is very important and intimidating, but we're going to get through it together.

Let's start where you should always start: your characters.

CHARACTER DEVELOPMENT

In the last chapter, we discussed the importance of having detailed and expansive background information for all of your characters. Specifics are key. Knowing them well will keep your ideas flowing and your story moving forward. Even if 90 percent of the information that you come up with for your characters doesn't wind up in the final product, this information is important, because it will inform you as a writer. Coming up with fun and creative backstories for your characters will also get your juices flowing!

Here are some different elements of character histories you might want to delve into when creating your story.

Hometown
Where your characters are from can affect many things about them, including the way they talk and the values they hold. The place they live might also say a lot about them. Are they in the same place they were born? Why? Do they live in a different place than where they were born? Why did they leave? Were they running from something or looking for a fresh start?

Family

One way or another, your parents are a huge part of shaping the person you become. Knowing the parents of your characters is as important as knowing any of the other characters. Are they strict disciplinarians or free-thinking hippies? Was your character raised in a religious home? What about your character's relationship with his or her sibling? Is your character an only child?

Culture

Cultural expectations are so deeply ingrained within us that we might not even realize it. Whether they are familial or societal, shaking your cultural expectations can be very difficult. Being a child of an immigrant family, for example, is going to affect the way your character goes about life. Is your character a first-generation or second-generation immigrant? How will this affect their choices and dreams? Does your character want to fight against culture? Will this lead to alienation from family and friends? Is your character trying to be the first of his or her family to go to college or leave home?

Age

The time when your characters are born and what generation they are a part of will also contribute greatly to their personality and public perception. Even the month of someone's birth can be used for their character. A character born on Christmas might have some issues, because they always feel that they are overlooked. Maybe parents treat their child differently because they are religious, and their child was born on Halloween or June 6, 2006 (6/6/06).

In another sense, living through certain periods, like 9/11, Pearl Harbor, or a large economic crisis, can affect the way your character approaches life. This might change his or her relational approach or

political views. Even facts like what TV shows and movies your character loved growing up can tell us a lot about him or her. It can also be a useful shortcut for letting the audience know your character's age without having to write it explicitly.

Name

There are a million different ways to come up with names for the characters in your movies. It might come to you as soon as you think of the character. You might spend hours trying to alter and perfect the names of everyone in your screenplay. Maybe you will just Google "popular tough guy names" to find ones that might fit your character. Names can often work as a quick indication of ethnic background or socioeconomic status as well.

Their histories

How do you reveal your characters' pasts without boring the audience? Try to let the information come out naturally, as the pace of the movie dictates. Do not rush to let the audience in on secrets, in the same way you wouldn't instantly tell a new friend all the hardships of your past. Most writers use big incidents or events to lead to truths coming out.

One famous example is *Thelma & Louise* (1991). In the movie, best friends Thelma and Louise head out of town for a weekend. Thelma meets a man in a roadside bar who tries to sexually assault her. After Louise catches him in the act, she winds up shooting him. Scared of what will happen, Louise convinces Thelma that they shouldn't go to the police. They go on the run, and Louise insists they go to Mexico. However, she refuses to go through Texas. Toward the end of the movie, you find out that she doesn't want to go through Texas because she was raped there in her past, and the perpetrators were never punished.

This past event informed her motivation for most of everything that she did in the rest of the movie. Would she have even shot the man if this hadn't happened? Would she have gone to the police? Would they have made it to Mexico without getting caught if they had gone through Texas? The movie is also made more suspenseful by her keeping her secret. It is more in keeping with her character and more truthful to the experience of a woman with serious trauma in her past.

Secrets can be difficult to manage, too. For example, a superhero's secret identity can often be tricky in regards to deciding which of his or her friends should and shouldn't know about it and whether or not it really keeps them safe. Try to decide what feels like the most honest and realistic way to keep and reveal secrets.

The Look of Your Characters

Describing characters in a screenplay is tricky. You do not want to describe the character in too much detail. This will bore the reader and cut the casting possibilities. For example, don't do this:

> Candy Adams is a 5'2" woman, originally from Atlanta, with long blonde hair and blue eyes. She is thin and attractive, wearing a red Donna Karan suit and matching Manolo Blahniks. Her bright smile lights up every party in town.

In your description, you should be trying to get to the heart of what is important about the character. If the things that are important to Candy are her southern roots and social status, it shouldn't matter if she's blonde or brunette or any color. Here's a better description:

> Candy Adams, 25, is a stylish, southern woman who loves God every bit as much as she does a good time.

With fewer specific appearance-based details, the director can have more room to put his or her vision forward. They might see Candy as a white, black, or Latina woman. You should try to leave appearance open to interpretation as much as possible.

Keeping track of it all

Once you decide on traits, characteristics, or historical facts about your characters, it is good to keep track of it all. Create note cards or a simple Word document with the background of each character. Being able to come back to your planning and research is important, as it will keep your writing schedule on track. You don't want to have to return to the planning stages when you're already deep into the writing process.

Secondary characters

It's all too easy for writers to treat secondary characters as throw-aways. How many movies have you seen where you don't even remember most of the friends because they're bland and fit into one of several clichés? The funny friend! The cool friend! The nervous, self-effacing friend! Here are a couple of tips to help you avoid these classic problems:

- **Minimize the amount of secondary characters in your story.** Instead of a group of friends, make it one or two. This will make it easier to give each character distinctive characteristics to make them memorable.
- **Make each character's voice distinct.** If your characters don't add anything to the story, you should strongly consider not including them at all.
- **Try to give your secondary characters equal amounts of screen time among themselves.**
- **Make sure each character is going on some kind of journey or transformation.** Every character in your movie should have an arc of some type, although your secondary characters will probably experience a less complicated one.

The_arc

One of the reasons that people might become bored with your movie is the lack of any kind of clear character arc. In addition to going on a journey to get what he or she wants, your character should be changing in some way and going on an internal journey.

Think of the Grinch. In *How the Grinch Stole Christmas*, he goes to Whoville to steal all the Christmas cheer from the Whos. But he winds up changing on the inside. As the story so famously puts it, his heart grew three sizes that day.

In *Jerry Maguire* (1996), Tom Cruise's character starts as a slick, fast-talking sports agent. Very early on, he has a breakdown and writes a mission statement about the way sports management should be. He knows he wants to be better, and he has to actually go out and make himself better. He quits his job, starts a new agency, works on his client Rod's career, and marries a woman. It's not until the end of the movie, when he is running to his wife and telling her that she completes him that we know he has truly changed.

Don't forget: your minor characters should be going on a journey during the film as well.

WRITING TO HELP UNDERSTAND YOUR CHARACTERS

Writing things that take place outside of your movie can actually be very helpful in getting your creative juices flowing. They may be scenes that you have zero intention of ever putting in the actual movie. But it can help you get a better grasp of character dynamics and voices, or it can shed light on the story in other ways. You could also potentially use these extra scenes later on as samples of your work or in marketing. You can even save parts to use again later on (maybe a sequel!).

Some settings you can place your characters in:

- Your protagonist and your romance character go fishing and come across a bear.
- One of your characters is Black Friday shopping and beating someone with a frozen pizza. He realizes he knows the person that he is beating with a frozen pizza.
- Two of your characters are helping your protagonist move into a new house.
- One of your characters is giving birth.
- Many of your characters are at the same Halloween party.
- One of your characters is taking a French cooking class.
- Two of your characters are at a running of the bulls.
- Your antagonist comes home to find a mysterious package at her door.
- Two of your characters are trapped in an elevator.
- Your antagonist is helping a woman who is having a baby.
- Your romance character is trying to get cast on a reality show.
- Your protagonist and reflection are eating lunch at McDonald's.
- Your antagonist is at a bank that is being robbed.
- Your romance character gets a haircut and hates it.
- Your protagonist is at the top of the Empire State Building.
- Your protagonist and your romance character are camping out for concert tickets.
- Your antagonist is on the first day at a new job.
- Your reflection is getting fired from a job.

CREATING STRUCTURE

When you sit down to write, with an idea ripe in your mind and a blank document in front of you, it can be hard to know where the story begins unless you know where it is going and what stops you want it to hit along the way. Having a solid structure and outline to your story is important if you want to get all of your points across to the audience.

Remember, you have to provide context, location, and story, but you also have to leave the work open to some interpretation by the director and actors.

A movie is like any other story, though. It will generally have a beginning, a middle, and an end. The beginning should draw viewers in, the middle should keep their attention, and the end should give them a satisfying resolution to the story and wrap up the subplots.

Three-act structure

You may be surprised to hear that pretty much every movie is structured in a three-act format. Since screenwriting guru Syd Field put a name to the technique, it has basically become the Hollywood standard. Once you learn about it, you'll have a hard time watching a movie and not noticing it.

The whole of your movie will be split into three acts, with a major plot point that serves as the turning point between each. Act 1 introduces the viewer to the movie. Act 2 is where the most action happens. Act 3 brings the movie to a satisfying close. We'll get more detailed in a second.

Movies are typically about 120 pages, or two hours long. The story can vary widely in length in either direction, but if you are a young screenwriter, you will want your story to be closer to 100 pages than 140. Studios will give less leeway to first-timers, and turning in something shorter will show the studio that you are able to edit your own work.

ASK THE EXPERT: "The first 10 pages of any screenplay are the most important. Almost everything you need to know about the movie is found in these first 10 pages. When the screenwriter sets up the first 10 pages of the screenplay, the reader must know immediately what's going on."
 — Syd Field, from his book "Four Screenplays"

Act 1: The set-up

The audience members have bought their tickets, grabbed their popcorn and drink, and sat through a seemingly endless amount of previews. They are ready to go on whatever journey you have laid out for them. In Act 1, they will see who and what the movie is about. Here, you will introduce them to the characters of your world and what they are trying to achieve.

The opening act of your screenplay should run until around page 30.

Let's use the opening act from *Bad Teacher* as an example. Cameron Diaz plays Elizabeth Halsey, a self-centered, irresponsible teacher. As the film opens, she is making a grand exit from John Adams Middle School to begin her life as a married woman. She stomps out to her Mercedes Benz and reverses in high speed away from the school, oblivious to the children standing nearby and the school bus that she cuts off. She hurls an insult at the school as she peels away. Throughout the movie, Elizabeth goes on to top herself, showing again and again that she is a bad teacher, but the opening scene lays out her character quickly. She is a self-centered, superficial person more concerned with labels and money than people and their feelings.

The first thing you see

The opening moments of a movie are critical to grabbing the viewer's attention. What scene do you want to set for the audience? Is your movie a lighthearted love story or a precisely paced thriller? How can you get the audience invested right from the start?

For instance, let's use the example of Emma and the grocery store that we mentioned earlier. Perhaps we would open that movie with shots of the grocery store, the generic suburban town, and a sign of how large the population is (perhaps by showing some teens lurking around a convenience store looking for trouble). At the beginning of the film, Emma might not take her job very seriously. To convey this, you might open the movie with a shot of Emma and Laura hiding in the meat freezer at the grocery store, eating a birthday cake they have stolen from the bakery department. Maybe Emma will say that they shouldn't be doing this. This will help us understand the setting and that we will be watching Emma's quest for a better job and a better life.

So, how do you write this?

The first 10 pages

Whether you like it or not, your first 10 pages will probably tell your reader everything they want or need to know about your screenplay. Here are some questions you should try to answer in those first 10 pages:

➡ Who are the people in your story? The main characters and important secondary characters should come into the film early unless the plot dictates otherwise. They have a lot to accomplish and need time to do it. The earlier you set things in action, the less likely the audience is to feel like the ending was rushed.

➡ Where do your characters live, work, and play? Give the audience an idea of who your characters are in their day-to-day lives. What are their daily routines? How will these routines change as the story progresses?

➡ What does your protagonist want? What journey is he or she going on? Why does he or she accept the challenge or chase the desire?

➡ What is he or she up against? Who is the antagonist, and why is he or she standing in the protagonist's way?

➡ What kind of movie is it? Set the tone. Will there be a lot of laughs, or will people want to pay close attention to every suspenseful moment?

This isn't to say that you should answer every question right off the bat. Give the audience a taste so they feel like they know what they're getting into. This gives you room creatively to find ways to keep them invested as well as surprise them. Make sure to also keep the locations of your scenes creative and visually interesting.

The first 10 pages are a great time to plant setups for later on as well. If your character is going to save himself from bad guys in the third act using well-developed kung fu skills, it might be a good idea to show him practicing (or mentioning) kung fu in the first 10 pages. Keep track of any potential setups, as the viewer may feel the story is unfinished if you leave certain threads hanging.

When you plant things in your screenplay, think of multiple ways you can pay them off. Look at Cady Heron's family in *Mean Girls*. At the beginning of the movie, Cady explains that she has spent her life in Africa because her parents were conducting field research. This makes her family incredibly out of touch with the day-to-day life of teenagers and the high school environment. This is paid off several times throughout the movie. Right away, we see Cady's parents send her off to school with advice better suited to a kindergartner than a high schooler. On Halloween, Cady is shocked by the revealing costumes the other girls are wearing. She frequently compares the rituals and interactions of high schoolers to those of animals she encountered in Africa.

Similarly, it is important to set up motivations for your characters. If the audience doesn't buy into the premise and why things are happening, they won't be invested in the journey. For example, the glimpse we get of Carl Allen (Jim Carrey) in the first 10 pages of *Yes Man* (2008) — divorced, ignoring friends and obligations, staying home alone and watching movies — helps convince us that he is the kind of person who would try to change his life by saying "yes" to every single new opportunity.

Don't forget that film is a visual medium. Any time you can use images rather than words to convey your idea, go for it. For example, if your movie has a character who lives in fear of a violent criminal, don't start the movie with that character saying, "I sure am scared of my neighbor Bill, the violent criminal." Show your character peering through his window at Bill, carefully going to his car in the morning, and locking all the doors and windows in the house to show his fear. Think of creative, visual ways to show things without having to write them out.

The event

This is the thing that sets your protagonist's journey into motion. It can also be referred to as the inciting incident or the catalyst. Maybe he or she learns a new piece of information that alters the course of his or her life. Maybe there is a call to action. Maybe something in your character's life needs fixing, and it can't wait any longer. Whatever the event is, it's something that will need to be dealt with immediately, thus setting the story into motion. This should take place around the tenth page and really get everything in your story rolling.

Plot point one

After the inciting incident, your story should quickly begin moving toward the first plot point (around page 30) where something happens that raises the stakes and pushes the story in a slightly different direction than the audience may have been expecting. The first plot point should affect the protagonist even more than the inciting event and should probably be a surprise to them.

This part functions as the unexpected drop in the roller coaster. Your protagonist will probably have been skipping along, completing the quest that started the whole thing without much pushback. Then, this point will come along and make the journey a little more complicated.

Act 2: The confrontation

Act 2 typically runs from about page 30 to page 70.

This is the part of the story where life undoubtedly becomes more difficult for your protagonist. The protagonist will have to prove they are passionate about whatever it is that they want. This section will include a bunch of smaller obstacles for the protagonist to overcome in order to get to the bigger one.

For example, if your protagonist is trying to become a star athlete, this part of the movie will include a lot of practicing, running up flights of stairs, waking up early to exercise, and putting in a lot of hard work behind the scenes.

Use this time to develop other characters and subplots as well. Make sure you set things up for the third and final act. If you want your character to run away to Brazil after a crime caper in the third act, make sure you plant the idea that he or she has always wanted to go to Brazil.

The second act is the hardest part of the movie to try to keep your audience's attention. One way to combat this is by making things more difficult for your protagonist. No one wants to watch a movie where nothing happens and everything goes exactly as planned. The problems in your protagonist's life should get worse as Act 2 progresses and builds toward the second plot point.

The Visual Medium

Always be thinking about what will be fun and exciting on the screen, the moments that people will remember and talk about with their friends later on. Think of unexpected and shocking things. Use the following film images to help brainstorm:

➡ The shot in *Star Wars: The Force Awakens* (2015) where the camera makes an inverted pan around the Millennium Falcon in mid-flight.

➡ The scene in *Furious 7* (2015) where a car jumps from one building into another building.

➡ The shot in *Avengers: Age of Ultron* (2015) where the super-heroes freeze in mid-air in positions that could have been taken straight from a comic book.

➡ The scene where the White House is destroyed by aliens in *Independence Day* (1996).

➡ The scene where the whale jumps over a boy and into the open water in *Free Willy* (1993).

These are the kinds of images and shots that will stick with you well after you leave the theater.

Plot point two

In this part, the stakes should be raised to their highest point, and the action should push the characters in yet another surprising direction. This time, our protagonist will either hit a new low or reach a new high — maybe even a false one. If there is a time element in your film, plot point two is a good time to remind the audience and add some pressure to the story. A classic example that you've probably seen is the kind where a character realizes he or she is in love with another character who is on their way to the airport to leave forever. He or she has to get there before the flight leaves!

Second act issues

Sustaining suspense throughout the middle of a story can be noto-riously difficult. The pacing of the movie can easily get screwed up because the second act is so much longer than the other two acts. Changing the tone or pacing of the movie too much can leave the audience feeling jarred and dissatisfied.

For instance, *Hancock* (2008) features Will Smith as an al-coholic superhero. As the movie begins, he saves an executive named Ray from being crushed by a train. This leads Ray to try to help Hancock rehabilitate his image. Ray's wife, Mary, still feels like most of the city distrusts Hancock. In the second act, the story changes dramatically after Mary reveals to Hancock that she is also a superhero and his former lover. The movie goes from being a dark comedy about a gruff superhero to being a romance about star-crossed lovers reuniting after 80 years apart. This confused many viewers, because they felt like they were watching two dif-ferent movies.

You also need to make sure that your protagonist is a constant presence in your second act, on screen or not, to ensure the tone of the movie stays steady. Don't go more than a couple scenes without addressing the main storyline.

Act 3: The resolution

Wrapping up your story is always going to be a difficult and unique challenge. The protagonist is bound to be at a turning point in his or her life. Your character will often take one last shot at the things that he or she wants. Sometimes, they will do so armed with new information or skills that they believe will make them successful. Other times, the protagonist will have no choice but to face the is-sue because someone else has confronted them with it.

The third act will include the climax and probably run from about page 70 to page 100. Make sure to leave room in the last few pages of your screenplay to wrap up any loose ends and ensure the audience will be satisfied that the story is resolved.

SCHADENFREUDE

Schadenfreude is a German word that refers to the pleasure one gets from seeing someone else's misfortune. The question is: Why is schadenfreude so prevalent in movies, and why do we enjoy watching other people suffer? The answer is still up for debate. Some research suggests people feel better about themselves after seeing the misfortunes of others. Audiences particularly seem to enjoy seeing someone get what he or she "deserves." Be careful, though. If you pile on the drama too thick, viewers will think your movie is too melodramatic or emotionally exaggerated. Let your characters dictate the way the story moves in a way that feels realistic to them.

CASE STUDY: RUNAWAY BRIDE

In case you're still a little confused by the three-act structure, let's take a look at an example to try and make it a little clearer. *Runaway Bride* is a big-budget romantic comedy from 1999. It makes for a good example, because its plot points are fairly easy to identify.

Opening image

Runaway Bride opens with the image the audience probably expected when they heard the movie's title: a bride on horseback, riding like someone who does not want to be caught. We know right away that this our main character. There is no need to verbally establish what is happening. The screenwriters trust that this glimpse of our beautiful heroine will pique our interest.

Then, the movie cuts away to introduce the other major character, Ike. As we see him go about his daily business, we learn many things about his character. He is a journalist with a weekly column. He is feeling particularly uninspired and in need of validation and encouragement. His friend doesn't pick up the phone, though, so Ike goes to a bar.

The event

While at the bar, Ike meets a guy who tells him about Maggie, the "runaway bride." We already know Ike is in desperate need of a story and lacking any particular motivation. So it is understandable that he would hear of the "runaway bride" and decide to write about her in his column. He winds up writing the story without almost any research in order to meet his deadline.

Plot point one

Maggie sends a scathing letter to the editor in response to Ike's column, pointing out that there are 15 errors in his story. This leads to Ike being fired from his job. This firing is the first plot point: It is unexpected for Ike, and it causes him to jump into action in a surprising way. After being offered the chance to get a byline in *GQ* and redeem himself, Ike begins tracking down Maggie to find the real story.

Act 2

In the second act, the audience begins to learn a lot about Maggie and Ike. We see her past weddings on tape, each with its own comic twist. In the first, Maggie storms right out of the church, dragging the ring bearer with her. The second wedding takes place at some kind of hippie wedding where Maggie jumps on a passing dirt bike to get away. The third one pays off the opening scene by showing the lead-up to her riding away on a horse. The groom of the third wedding turns out to be the mysterious man from the bar who tipped off Ike.

There is also a meeting and a great amount of interaction between Maggie and Ike in the second act. Maggie and her friend Peggy dye Ike's hair while feeding him bad information. Maggie has a luau in a barn. We learn that one of the near-grooms is now a priest. Maggie's grandmother comments on Ike's appearance. Maggie gets engaged again, with the wedding date fast approaching.

It becomes clear that the climax of the story will probably occur at this wedding.

Then, Ike points out to Maggie that she seems to be confused about who she really is. For instance, he says, she doesn't even know how she likes her eggs, because she always orders the same breakfast as her fiancé. By the time Maggie's fourth wedding rehearsal rolls around at the midpoint of the movie, Maggie and Ike realize they are in love. She breaks up with her latest groom-to-be, and the audience is treated to scenes showing Ike and Maggie spending time together and falling in love.

Since there is a wedding and a date already booked, they decide to try to get married. Ike is confident because he thinks he has gotten to know the Maggie that none of the other guys even tried to know. He is convinced that she will make it to the altar for him.

Plot point two

It's the day of the wedding. For the fifth time, Maggie is trying to make it down the aisle. This time, reporters are outside, clamoring for shots of the once-cynical and dismissive Ike, preparing to marry the "runaway bride."

As Maggie makes her way down the aisle, she keeps steady eye contact with Ike. This try will be successful. This is the marriage that counts. Then, as someone takes a picture, the flash causes Ike to close his eyes. At that moment, Maggie turns and runs. Ike chases her through the church, across a children's classroom, and out of a window before jumping on a FedEx truck that takes her away. Ike runs behind it, screaming her name, embarrassing and humiliating himself in front of his former colleagues.

As the second act comes to a close, it feels like all is lost. Maggie has run away again, making Ike into a national laughingstock. His face is on the front of his former paper. The audience is left to wonder how this could possibly be fixed.

Act 3

Here, we finally see Maggie trying to take charge of her life. She confronts her father about his teasing and begins to design and sell lamps. We see her trying different kinds of eggs to determine which she likes. Thanks to these events, when we see her return to Ike, we know that she has changed.

The climax

Ike comes across Maggie, waiting in his apartment to tell him about the changes she has made for the better. She tells him how she likes her eggs and turned in her running shoes. She pops the question. This time, the audience knows the wedding will last.

Conclusion

At a small wedding with only their closest friends in attendance, Ike and Maggie are finally married. We see the townspeople celebrating. Ike and Maggie share one last kiss, and the film fades to black.

Subplots

Most of the subplots in *Runaway Bride* involve Maggie's friends and family and her relationship with them. Let's detail a few of them here:

Maggie's father and his alcoholism.
This subplot begins in the second act, when Ike sees Maggie picking up her dad from the bar, because he is too drunk to drive. It resolves in Act 3 when Maggie confronts her father and tells him that while he might not like having a daughter with commitment issues, she doesn't like having a drunk for a father. The point seems to resonate. The issue isn't completely resolved, but he and the family finally seem ready to deal with his problem.

Maggie's relationship with her best friend Peggy.
Peggy is endlessly cheerful and supportive. Seeing their relationship through Ike's eyes, Maggie comes to realize that she hasn't always been the best friend to Peggy.

Maggie as the town laughingstock.
Ike originally contributes to this problem, but eventually, he realizes that Maggie is hurt by the way she is treated at the town bridal shop and during her luau, where the guests roast her about her past. This storyline is resolved in the last few minutes of the movie as we see the town celebrating the climactic wedding.

Your screenplay can have multiple subplots as long as they are well-developed and don't detract from the main story. While working with subplots, don't forget to check back in with the main storyline frequently. If possible, advance the subplots along with the main storyline. For instance, when Maggie and Ike get married, it simultaneously moves along the subplot regarding Maggie's reputation in the town.

Breaking from the three-act structure

Many successful movies have attempted to subvert the classic three-act structure in their storytelling. A good example is Christopher Nolan's cult classic *Memento* (2000). Nolan, who has gone on to direct big-budget movies like *Inception* and *The Dark Knight*, crafted *Memento* with his brother Jonathan Nolan.

The movie tells the story of a man with retrograde amnesia who wakes up every morning as a completely blank slate. He has been this way since his wife's murder, and he spends his days trying to investigate and avenge her death, which is difficult since he forgets everything about himself and his situation every time he wakes up. He has adapted some techniques to keep his investigation going, including tattooing every inch of his body with words and numbers relevant to his investigation and taking Polaroids of everyone he interacts with to remember who is an ally and who isn't. The movie is told partially in chronological order and partially in reverse to give the viewer a taste of what it is like to have the main character's condition. This peculiar way of presenting the plot forces viewers to pay close attention to the film in order to recognize any semblance of a traditional narrative structure.

Another movie that attempts to defy convention is the German film *Run Lola Run* (1998). The story technically follows a three-act structure, but it upends traditional movie storytelling methods by effectively playing the entire story out three times with three different endings.

The movie opens with the main character Lola getting a call from her boyfriend Manni. He needs her to get $100,000, money he owes a drug dealer but somehow left on a subway car. Manni says he needs the money within 20 minutes or else he will rob a grocery store. Lola decides to ask her father, who is a bank manager, for the money. She tells Manni not to do anything. She hangs up the phone and runs down the stairs. This is the divergence point of the movie. When it begins playing out the second and third versions of the story, this is the point where the story picks back up from.

The first time, Lola runs to her father's bank to ask for the money. He refuses and tells Lola that he is sick of his marriage, sick of her mother, and sick of her because she isn't even really his child. Shaken up, Lola joins Manni in robbing the store, and she is shot by a police officer.

Then, the film returns back to the divergence point. The second time, Lola is tripped by a dog on the way down the staircase. She stumbles upon her father talking to his mistress and robs the bank in a fit of rage. She gets away with the money, but Manni is killed as he crosses the street to meet her.

Then, back again. The third and final time, Lola runs faster than ever before. Manni finds the homeless guy who picked his money up from the subway car and trades him his gun for the bag. In this last reality, Lola and Manni survive and walk away with the money.

CREATING AN OUTLINE

The three-act structure is difficult to follow if you don't have any, well, structure. If you don't take the time to sit down and create a detailed outline for your script, writing is going to be much harder than you expect.

Outlining can be intimidating. When you only have about two hours to work with, wrangling a complicated story that involves several characters and their journeys can be a real challenge. If you don't properly lay out the reasons and ways that characters reach their conclusions, you risk leaving the audience feeling unfulfilled.

You need an outline that's easy to follow, easy to tinker with, and easy to transport. It should also allow you to take either a birds-eye or molecular view of your story at any time.

The easiest system to implement and follow is the index card system. Each card gives a snapshot of a scene in the movie. Looking at the index card should tell you where the scene takes place, which characters are involved, and the major action the scene accomplishes for the overall plot. Each time your characters change location, begin a new card.

Once all of your scenes are outlined and have their own card, figure out how they are going to fit together. This helps you break down what looks like a huge task into one that is much more manageable. If you outline well, the transition into the actual writing process will be quick and seamless. Write one scene a day (usually two or three pages), and your first draft will be done in a month and a half.

You might want to get a board or flat surface to pin or tape your cards to so you can see your whole story as you work on outlining and writing. The high points. The low points. The subplots and how they are wound in. Surveying all of the cards will make it easy to see the pacing of the action, where the story begins and ends, and how everything is being woven together.

UNVERIFIED ADVICE: "By failing to prepare, you are preparing to fail."
— Benjamin Franklin, Founding Father

"Give me six hours to chop down a tree and I will spend the first four sharpening the axe."

      – Abraham Lincoln, 16th President of the United States

"If you don't know where you are going, you'll end up someplace else."

    – Yogi Berra, baseball player, Hall-of-Famer

Making the cards

The story card process should be a stage where you indulge yourself and have some fun. Come up with all kinds of entertaining scenes, and try to figure out what will fit in to the story. You probably won't have every scene of the movie in mind already, but as you plan things out and pin things to the board, you'll find that things will continuously pop into your mind and spark more and better ideas.

Don't be too critical of your own ideas at this stage. You still have plenty of time to mold them and unearth better ones as you work through the writing process.

Across the top of each card, write the scene location information. Remember, INT is for interior or inside, and EXT is for exterior or outside. Follow that with the actual location (i.e. GRANDMA'S HOUSE) and whether the scene is taking place during DAY or NIGHT.

Next, write a synopsis of just the most important part of the scene. What does it accomplish in the overall action of the film? Don't include many details. Keeping the cards as simple as possible is important so you can switch the overall order as you lay things out.

Here's an example of what a story card might look like for the grocery store movie about Emma:

INT-DELI COUNTER-DAY

Emma finds out about the open manager position.

In this scene, Emma might arrive at work, feeling particularly lazy. She might clock in and find out she is working the deli counter alone. She doesn't usually work the position and has no idea where anything is. She might hear about the open manager position while helping a customer and eavesdropping on her boss. None of these details would appear on the index card.The only thing that "matters" in this scene is that Emma finds out about the new job posting. The other stuff makes the scene interesting, but this is the information that will push the story forward.

Once you have your whole story thought out, make a story card for each plot point you know you will need for the movie to make sense. Think of the things that you cannot afford to leave out.

Subplots
At their best, subplots and secondary characters will add pieces to the puzzle, painting a fuller image for the audience to consider. They should provide a slightly different take on things.

You might want to simply list the subplot right underneath the main story when you're working on a story card. If you feel they are important enough, though, give the subplots their own card.

Here are some questions to think about as you create subplots:
- How are the events presented in the subplot different than those in the main plot? The subplot should complement the main storyline without echoing it exactly.

☞ How often does the subplot retell a situation presented in the main plot? Subplots should tie into things happening to the main character without replaying moments that the audience has already seen.

☞ How is the viewer's experience heightened by this plotline? Some subplots put the audience in a superior position where they know things the character does not.

☞ Does the subplot have a distinctive beginning, middle, and end? The subplot needs to resolve itself just as any main plot might, whether it is halfway through the movie or at the very end.

Conflict

Movies are made up of a series of conflicts. Each scene should have a conflict at its heart. If you are having a hard time identifying the conflict in each scene, consider what is motivating each character. What does each person want in the scene? What can they achieve or gain?

Always be thinking about what your characters want out of any particular moment, large or small. Try to identify the conflict on each of your cards.

Marking the cards

Once you have many of your cards laid out, you may want to mark them to make things easier to follow. Many screenwriters will mark the cards with various colors of dots, checkmarks, and other symbols representing specific things. For example, a card where the romantic subplot is advanced might be marked with a heart or red dot. Other writers like to mark cards with letters or initials of characters featured in the scene. Others might mark the cards based on conflict and its resolution, as well as the emotional changes of the characters in the scene. Having an organizational system like this will make it easy to go back and make sure every subplot is carried out well and every character is treated fairly.

Creating the board

Find a bulletin board or flat surface that can accommodate your cards well. Thumbtacks work well for putting up the cards, as you can also take the cards down and put a rubber band around them whenever you need to store them. When you take them down, you might want to use an indexing or numbering system to make things easier when revising scenes in later writing stages.

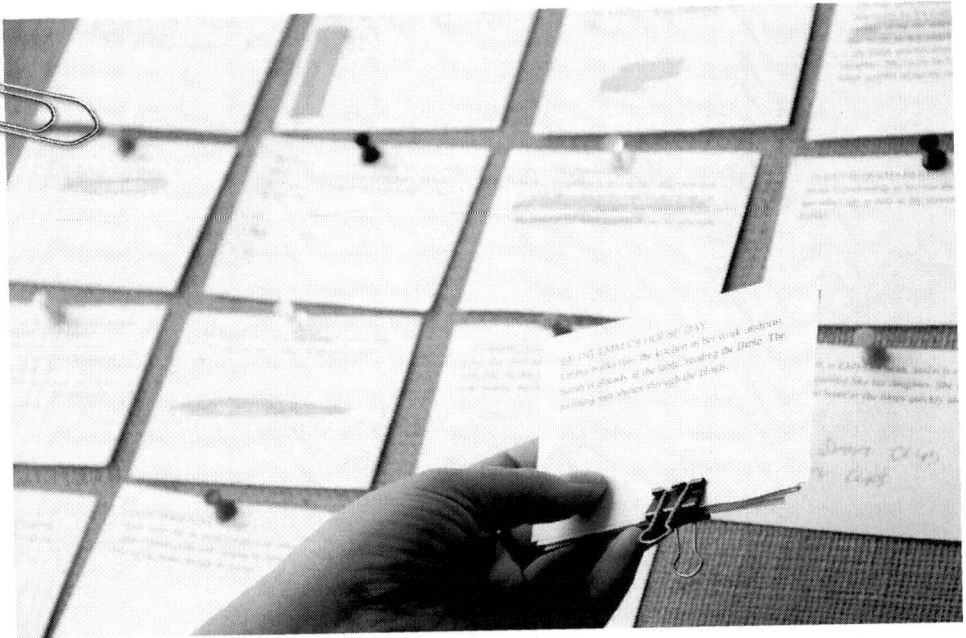

Your board should have four rows, listed as Act 1, Act 2, Act 2, and Act 3. Place these title cards on the far left-hand side of the board.

ACT 1 — The scenes from the beginning up to plot point one.

ACT 2 — This row runs from the beginning of Act 2 to the midpoint of the film.

ACT 2 — The third row (and second row for Act 2) should run from the movie's midpoint to the end of the second act.

ACT 3 — Act 3: The last row will contain the scenes that happen from the beginning of Act 3 until the end of the movie.

Each row should be about 10 cards long. Remember to give yourself a little space and allow flexibility, as your plans will surely change as the writing process goes along. You want to create a solid framework, but you also want to allow yourself room to play creatively.

As you look over your cards, make sure that the scenes seem to be building toward something. You want your cards to function like dominoes, where one scene inevitably falls smoothly into the next. The events of each card should depend on events of previous cards. When everything is planned out like this, your writing process will be much smoother.

The board can also be helpful when examining your movie's pacing. If there are 10 cards in the first row and only six in the second, it might mean Act 2 is moving too slowly. Make sure if you have large shifts in pacing it is intentional. Always make sure your action is moving forward.

Common script problems

Story cards will also help you keep track of different storytelling elements throughout the screenplay. Here are a few you might run into:

➡ **Setups:** The board will make it easy to see what has happened so far and what still needs to happen. This will help keep you from leaving plot points hanging. Take note of all the things that need to take place in order for your endings to work. Make sure each situation is set up properly. If you need a gun in the third act, be sure to show it in the first one.

➡ **Character Arcs:** The story cards also make it easy to track each character's personal development. Every character in your movie should be going on a journey, and their paths have to make sense. Not everyone will change at the same rate, but you need to have your characters learn something or change in some way during your story. The board will help you maintain a birds-eye view of every character and the ways they change during the movie.

➡ **Subplots:** Having the ability to look at the number of subplot scenes you have set aside from the primary story will make things easier to balance. There is no particular ratio of subplot to main plot that you should shoot for, but you'll be able to feel things out better by laying it out. The most important thing is that your subplots don't tilt the balance of your story unevenly in their direction.

ASK THE EXPERT: "You can't fix a bad script after you start shooting. The problems on the page only get bigger as they move to the big screen."

— Howard Hawks, screenwriter and filmmaker during the classic Hollywood era (1920s through 1960s)

ESTABLISHING VOICE

Alright, so here you are. You've done a lot of planning. You've laid out a story, sketched out some characters, and built your board full of story cards.

Now comes, arguably, your biggest challenge. How do you write in a way that people actually talk while simultaneously establishing your own voice as a writer? This can sound intimidating. People can talk in all kinds of different ways. Some people are constantly formulating the exact right way to say things. Others are babbling on, trying to be the funniest person in the room.

ASK THE EXPERT: "To gain your own voice, you have to forget about having it heard."

— Allen Ginsberg, 20th century poet

When writing your characters, think about what their social style would be, the way they would speak, the images they would hope to project, and what their motivations would be in any given scene.

Dialogue should also always have a purpose in advancing the plot. Be careful about this purpose being too obvious, though. You have to find a way for your characters to put forth their own voices and agendas while advancing the plot you carefully devised. Keep all of your dialogue short and to the point, and think about how it will translate onto the screen.

When you first start writing, you might find that each character has the same voice: yours. It's hard to talk like someone else, let alone several different people. Focus mainly on getting your ideas on the page in the early drafting process. You can chisel away and make each voice more distinctive and personality-filled as you revise and get further into the writing process.

Let's look at a few different ways that you can make your characters pop off the page in your script.

Verbal sparring

There should be some kind of conflict driving each scene. Each character should always want something, and something else should be standing in the way. Think of their words as the only weapons they have to do battle.

As your characters fight for what they want, one character might lead the conversation while the other follows. The leading character might be playing with the other person, enjoying the power of knowing a secret. Look at this example:

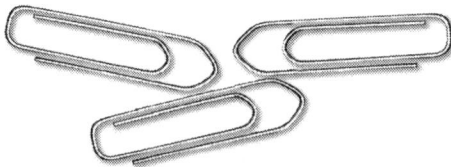

INT-LIVING ROOM-DAY

                    RUTH
            I talked to Jack.

                    LANCE
            Why would you do that?

                    RUTH
        Jack says that he saw you on Friday.

                    LANCE
        Jack doesn't know what he saw.

                    RUTH
            Where were you on Friday?

                    LANCE
    Where I said I was the last time you asked. Did
                you see Jack?

                    RUTH
            We just talked.

                    LANCE
            On the phone?

                    RUTH
            We just talked.

                    LANCE
            Did you see him?

                    RUTH
    I just wanted to know the truth, once and for all.

                    LANCE
            Did you go to his house?

                    RUTH
    I never would've had to if you'd told me the
                    truth!

In movies, "beats" are the points where the energy in a scene shifts from one character to another. Your scenes should be made up of a series of beats. Identifying them and counting them out can be very helpful to the writing process. Find the specific energy that is going along with each beat. This will help you know when to shift it and change up the way characters are speaking.

Look at the last example. Try to identify the moments where the power and energy is shifting between the characters.

Make sure you are also thinking about how much dialogue you are using for each character. In a two-person back-and-forth, for instance, be careful to avoid long monologues where one person speaks uninterrupted for minutes at a time. Have you ever been in a social situation where you were able to talk for that long uninterrupted?

Nonverbal cues

The things your characters say with their body language are just as important as the things they say with words. You can write entire scenes without dialogue, using just nonverbal cues. The audience is smart enough to absorb the implications of nonverbal cues, and this can be all the more powerful. The scene can just be about the way your two romantic characters look at each other from across the room, the monotony of a typical morning routine, or the sights your character sees on the way to work.

Remember, you shouldn't be giving long stage directions because the actors have a job to do as well. Write short and simple descriptions that leave room for your actors to play.

Subtext

Even more so than nonverbal cues, the words left unsaid between characters can be critically important. Your characters might not be able to fully express themselves. Secrets might simmer just under the surface of the story. These things are all subtext, the part of the conversation that makes you think something is up with a certain character or group of characters. Subtext can be words left unsaid or words that mean much more than they seem to at face value. It helps create tension and suspense in a scene.

Let's use a simple example: Say your boss calls you by the wrong name. You might not want to say anything about it so you don't embarrass him or her. Maybe you'll be really offended. Or maybe you'll act rude or sarcastic for the rest of the day. You won't say any of these reasons, but they will be very clear below the surface. This is subtext.

Think of the different ways your character can convey how damaged she is from her mother's alcoholism. She won't say, "I wish you hadn't missed my swim meets because you were always too drunk to drive." She'll be vaguer, saying something like, "I wish you hadn't missed my swim meets." The unspoken reason for this will hang between the characters, creating weight and tension. Maybe she'll say, "Anna Thompson's mom and sister went to every swim meet. They even made signs on poster board," and then trail off. This is a more complete and specific memory that paints a vibrant picture and adds more subtext. The audience will understand that it hurt your character as a child to have to watch one of her teammates with her perfect family while she sat alone.

If your dialogue is too on-the-nose, like "I wish you hadn't missed my swim meets because you were always too drunk to drive," the audience won't believe your characters. Let their real intentions and meanings come through the words they speak about other topics. Treat them like normal humans.

Exposition

Exposition is the part of the dialogue designed to inform or remind the viewer about something they need to know. For example, in a heist movie, the audience will need to understand how the actual heist is supposed to go, because something will probably go wrong.

The difficulty with exposition is that it's not typically the most interesting thing to watch. You might want to have something stimulating going on visually to keep the audience interested, like showing how the heist is supposed to go in a montage while your character is explaining the plan.

If you feel the audience needs reminding about a scene from earlier in the movie, think of a way that you can call back to the incident. Let's say that your protagonist is Annie, whose house burned down two weeks ago. To give the audience an idea of how much time has passed, you might want to bring this up. Tuck this old event into a story that moves the plot forward. For example, you might have Annie's mom inquire into the status of Annie's insurance claim:

> ANNIE'S MOM
> Have you spoken to the insurance company?
>
> ANNIE
> Not yet.
>
> ANNIE'S MOM
> Why not? It's been two weeks.
>
> ANNIE
> I just can't deal with it yet.

This helps remind the viewer of the fire, but it also pushes the story toward her meeting with the insurance company while also revealing a little bit about both Annie and her mother.

CASE STUDY: FIVE ESSENTIAL SCREENWRITING TIPS

Zondra Wilson
Writer and Actress
www.twitter.com/zondrawilson
www.instagram.com/zondrawilson
www.facebook.com/zondrawilson

It's understandable if you are feeling nervous about the thought of writing a screenplay. The rules! The formatting! The binding! It can appear to be overwhelming. But, actually, it's not, Don't let the seemingly endless parade of screenwriting elements scare you away from writing your first script. Here are five tips to make sure your screenplay is the best it can be.

1. Establish and maintain a clear voice

In a well-written play, each character has his or her own speech pattern. Some may ramble, others may have a lisp, while some speak as if they graduated Summa Cum Laude from an Ivy League School. If they all sound alike, none feel genuine and the audience senses a disconnect.

Likewise, our voice — our character, if you will — should not sound like everyone else. We may admire the way another person writes, but if we emulate too closely, we rob readers of diversity and run the risk of presenting only a stale copy.

If we are writing a work that requires more than one voice (unless the script calls for it), we should be careful that no given speaker flips back and forth between sounding like two different people. Each voice should be distinct and consistent to ensure fluidity and credibility.

2. Speak in vernacular

Characters on a stage need to convey their personalities through the way they speak, and the more natural the speech is, the more accessible the character.

Depending on the venue, grammar rules can — and ought — to be flexible.

In casual writing, following stuffy and prescriptive rules feels like legalese, not a blog post from a friend.

Intentional disregard for a rule can create a timing or mood effect that enhances the writing. Conscious use of fragments, for example, can direct pacing or add emphasis. And it's how people talk.

A word of caution: "natural" is not the same thing as "sloppy."

It's a mistake to think that grammatical conventions are unimportant. They provide clarity. A communication world without proper punctuation gets messy and confused very quickly.

Thus, we need to know the rules of grammar well enough to know when and how we can break them.

3. Give stage directions

In a script, there are often cues given to the actors as to how they should say their line:

[Sadly], [Hesitating], [While falling off the desk].

Sometimes, we need to tell our readers how to "hear" the lines we are delivering. In casual writing, this usually involves things like bolds, italics, or CAPS.

These tools, like the tweaks in grammar, aid in a sense of timing or emphasis, which in turn help convey the intended mood.

That said, we can overuse these tools easily. We should write the first draft with it, and then read it aloud to find out where the natural words of emphasis are.

4. Show, don't tell
Although it is occasionally necessary to have a narrator explain what's going on in a play, that's usually deemed as a cop-out for a scriptwriter. Audiences should ideally be able to pick up on the context from the dialog and action.

A well-placed line can give attentive listeners information about the past and clues about the future.

We need to paint the story of growth and self-realization through the events and images in our writing. Our readers are smart enough. They'll figure it out. We can get our message across without stating and restating the obvious.

5. Leave 'em hanging
Well-crafted scripts make sure that questions are left unanswered and conflicts left unresolved at the end of each act so that the audience will keep coming back for more.

When this happens, the audience is sucked in and wouldn't dream of moving from their seats. They want to see what happens next.

Zondra Wilson is a business owner, actress, and writer who made her television debut in 2006 with a guest starring role as a newscaster on the CBS hit daytime soap opera "The Young and The Restless." She has written two screenplays: "The Senator's Wife" and "On the Brink." Zondra is also a former television news/sports anchor and reporter.

CHAPTER 5:

BEGINNINGS AND ENDINGS

In every moment of your screenplay, you should be trying to keep your audience's attention, to make them want to watch the next scene or turn to the next page. Still, beginnings and endings might require a little extra attention, because those are the most crucial parts of the movie. The beginning helps the audience decide if they want to keep watching. The ending will be the taste that stays in their mouths when they leave the theater.

We briefly covered beginnings and endings in Chapter 4, but it's time to get more specific. Let's talk about what your beginnings and endings need for your movie to be a success.

THE BEGINNING

The beginning will set the tone and pace for your film. The key is making sure you pique the audience's curiosity with your opening. Many movies are full of action and will want to open with an attention-grabbing scene like an argument or a chase. This approach would probably be ill-advised, though, if your film was a quieter, family feature. Try to find an image that represents what your movie is actually about. The key is finding an opening that fits your movie and raises questions that the story will set out to answer.

Introducing your movie
If your movie is like a roller coaster, think of your protagonist as the audience's car on that coaster. Once it is clear to them who the protagonist is, they will know that the ride is really about to start. This will settle the audience nicely into the events of the film. The sooner you can get the hero on screen, the better. If your movie opens with a group scene, find a way to distinguish the main character in some way.

For instance, *Miss Congeniality* (2000) starts with a quick scene that shows the main character, Gracie Hart, as a child, being a tough tomboy who tries to help others and regularly gets ridiculed for her efforts. When the film jumps forward in time to an FBI sting, it is obvious to the audience which character is Gracie, because she is one woman on a team of men, still being ridiculed and belittled for her earnest efforts. Make sure your audience knows who to focus on.

Establish or allude to any important relationships early on — sidekicks, best friends, romantic interests, family — if they are crucial to setting up the main plot and everything else that is going to happen.

Flipping to page 10

If your reader isn't hooked by page 10, your script isn't working.

At this point, all of the setup should be in place, the picture of your protagonist's life should be fairly well-developed, and the inciting incident that sets everything in motion should be happening or should already have happened. Think of it this way: If your scenes average a length of two pages, you have five scenes to set up the movie. Ten minutes. If the action hasn't started unraveling by this point, your movie may wind up feeling rushed (or worse yet, way too long).

Let's take a look at how we might be able to use the first five scenes to set up the movie about Emma and the grocery store:

➡ **Opening:** Emma and Laura are at work, slacking off. The scene shows Emma's current job, her attitude, and her friendship with Laura.

➡ **Scene 2**: Emma throws a brunch for her friend. This scene highlights how small of a town she lives in and shows how most of its people marry and start families very young.

➡ **Scene 3**: Emma hears friends gossiping about her. This shows that her friends are insincere and only hang out with her for superficial reasons.

➡ **Scene 4**: Emma tries and fails to confide in her mom. The scene shows how fragile Emma's relationship with Sarah is and could potentially introduce Sarah's alcoholism as well.

➡ **Scene 5**: Emma goes out and drinks too much so that she doesn't have to think about her very bad day. This makes it clear to the audience that Emma is not ready to confront the difficult problems she is facing in her life.

By page 10, Emma will be returning to work at her lowest point. Then, she will hear about the open manager position, setting the movie up for not just her primary goal of attaining the job, but her secondary and more emotionally resonant goal of taking control of her life.

THE MACGUFFIN

Have you heard the term "MacGuffin" before? Because you've almost definitely seen one. In storytelling, a MacGuffin is a motivating element that doesn't actually serve any purpose. While a plot device drives the story, a MacGuffin is what the story is driving toward. Think of it this way: In a heist story, it doesn't really matter if the criminals are going after the Mona Lisa or a fancy diamond. The rest of the story would pretty much be the same. The object being pursued in those cases is a MacGuffin. If you've seen a movie in-

volving a storyline like "Hurry! We must find this thing before *they* do!" you've seen a MacGuffin.

For instance, the classic film *Pulp Fiction* uses a briefcase that all the characters are chasing as a MacGuffin. Every character is trying to get it, and there is no particular reason why. MacGuffins typically have meanings that are unexplained and left open to interpretation by viewers. Frankly, their meaning may have not been thought out at all by the artists.

ENDING

Writing an ending that you are satisfied with is an incredible challenge. Writing an ending that your entire audience is satisfied with is a near impossibility. It's one thing to have to try to wrap up all of your plot into a cohesive and logical ending, but it's another thing entirely to make it compelling and surprising at the same time.

ASK THE EXPERT: "Great is the art of the beginning, but greater is the art of the ending."
      – Henry Wadsworth Longfellow, 19th century author and poet

There are two important elements you need to focus on when it comes to your ending: the climax that resolves the main storyline, and the final scenes that wrap everything up nicely.

The climax

The part of the movie when your main story is resolved is called the climax. It is not the end of the movie. There should be time after the climax to tie off any loose ends, and you should still have the opportunity to send the audience home with a particular message or feeling.

In Emma's story, the climax would probably take place when the company announces who received the managerial promotion. That is the moment that will resolve the film's central journey. The movie will not fade to black the moment that Emma finds out whether she won the position or not. There should be other threads and subplots that still need to be tied up (what happens between Emma and her love interest, whether Laura and the baker start a romance, how Sarah's alcoholism fares, etc.).

Here's what a card for the climactic scene might look like:

```
INT-MANAGER'S OFFICE-DAY

Emma finds out she is the new manager.
```

Meanwhile, there are several other scenes that could still round out the movie.

EXT-GROCERY STORE
PARKING LOT-DAY

Dave confronts Emma.

She admits she got the
job.

Dave breaks up with
Emma.

INT-EMMA'S HOUSE-NIGHT

Emma tells Sarah about
the promotion.

Sarah asks Emma to
promise that she won't
work at a grocery
store her whole life.

INT-MANAGER'S
OFFICE-DAY

Emma turns down the
job.

EXT-PARKING LOT-DAY

Dave asks Emma if she wants
to get back together.

She says no. Drives away in
her car, which is packed
with all her stuff.

As she drives out of town,
she honks at Laura and
the new baker, who are
passionately kissing.

Working backward

If you are struggling to write an ending, you might want to try to envision the last scenes of the movie first and work backward from there. Think about the image you want to leave viewers with, and consider what beats you need to hit to reach that point.

Be careful of this approach, though. You don't want to get so caught up trying to write an awesome ending that the rest winds up not making any sense.

Turning convention on its head

You should also be wary of trying to create a surprising twist in your ending. Many times, forcing a surprise ending upon the story can ruin the ending completely. The surprise has to come naturally from the story. If you are trying to shock the audience just for the sake of doing so, they will come away feeling cheated.

Similarly, stacking one surprise on after another may rob the audience of their ability to feel surprised and make the movie completely ridiculous. For example, the movie *Knowing* (2009) is about a young boy who experiences a number of strange predictions. The movie closes with a ridiculous number of twists and turns. The father realizes his son has the ability to predict natural disasters and their corresponding deaths. The boy reveals that the world is going to end and everyone will die. Aliens come and take the boy to a new planet to start over. The dad lets his son go and waits alone for the world's fiery end.

Each of these events on their own might sound a little ridiculous but would probably still stand up to audience scrutiny. However, the more twists and turns you stack on top of each other, the more overwhelmed and willing to bail on the movie the audience will become.

Try to think of organic ways to surprise your audience. For instance, if they have been following one specific character's point of view throughout, it would make more sense when a surprise came in through a different character. It's a challenge to write, no doubt, particularly if you are intentionally limiting the audience's view of the overall story, but it could make the "surprise" more effective.

A classic example of this would be *The Sixth Sense* (1999), since you only see things from the protagonist's point of view until the twist ending. When he is caught by surprise, so are we.

CHAPTER 6:

DEVELOPING THEME

Some people are interested in more than just a well-told, captivating story. They might enjoy breaking movies down on more profound levels. For a movie to be successful and worth revisiting, they might prefer some kind of strong subtext or deeper meaning behind the events happening on-screen. An entire field — film criticism — is based off this kind of thinking.

For example, a critical movie fan might say that *Whiplash* (2014) is much more than just a story of a young man trying to be the best drummer in the world. Rather, you might say it is a commentary on what it takes to be a successful person in the world, on how hard you should work if you really want something, on the virtues and drawbacks of tough love. These are themes, the subjects that movies are "really about." Themes can be mottos or life lessons you want your audience to take away from your film, or simply questions that you want to bring up.

You might write your entire first draft without thinking about the deeper meaning of your screenplay. In revision, though, you should really begin to think about the themes and messages your movie is conveying and make sure to highlight and emphasize them.

ASK THE EXPERT: "To produce a mighty book, you must choose a mighty theme."
     – Herman Melville, author of "Moby Dick"

Let's use Emma and our grocery store script as an example. You have a charming story about a woman who wants to overcome her circumstances and make a better life. You might think it's just a romantic comedy without any particular message. But like it or not, even the screwiest of screwball comedies will have some kind of message at the heart of its story. In this case, the story is one of

Emma being more limited by her own expectations and decisions than she is by her actual life circumstances. Over the course of the movie, Emma will attempt to steer herself down a different and more fulfilling path. The moral of the story could wind up being many different things, depending on which themes you emphasize.

➡ **You can achieve your dreams, no matter what people think.** Emma can succeed at anything when she puts her mind to it. She gets the job, gets the guy, and flies off into her glamorous new life.

➡ **You are limited only by the restrictions you put on yourself.** After Emma triumphs over her obstacles, she realizes that the only thing standing in her own way was herself. Laura gets up the nerve to approach the bakery guy and discovers he is equally crazy about her. Sarah gets over her stage fright and sings beautifully. Her fear was the only thing stopping her from staying sober and succeeding.

➡ **Your relationships — not material success — are what make life worth living.** Emma does not get the promotion, but during the course of her journey, she grows closer to her mother, her new love interest, and Laura. She realizes that living a fuller life in her hometown is just as satisfying as moving and starting completely over.

There are all kinds of messages you can take away from your screenplay. The way you set up the story, the views you give your characters, and the outcome of your hero's journey are all things that contribute to this message. You shape these aspects of the message to match the vision you have as a writer.

The Greek Chorus

In ancient Greek plays, conveying theme was typically easier thanks to the chorus. The chorus was typically a couple of characters who appeared onstage with the players, offering commentary and backstory for the audience. Many modern works include some form of this, like a character that breaks the fourth wall and speaks to the audience, offering criticism, opinion, or clarification. Here are some examples:

➡ Statler and Waldorf in the Muppet TV shows and movies (the two cranky guys in the balcony) frequently make sarcastic comments about whatever the Muppets are doing.

➡ Timon and Pumbaa, Simba's sidekicks in *The Lion King*, offer the film's young audience an insight into something they might not otherwise pick up on when Timon explains to an oblivious Pumbaa that Simba and Nala are falling in love.

➡ The singer and guitar player in *There's Something About Mary* (1998) explain our main character, Ted, and his undying love for Mary, his high school crush. They appear at other points in the movie, reiterating that Mary is the only girl for Ted.

HOW TO DEVELOP THEME

As we've said, your primary and secondary themes might not even come to you when you are first writing your screenplay. You might have to look through everything after you finish to see what common ideas are running through your story. Think about the message the reader is getting. What lessons will they take away? What sort of things will they be thinking about when they leave the theater?

Even if you don't want to give the audience direct answers to things, you still need to ask questions. Maybe your movie will take more of an "is cheating wrong?" vibe than a "cheating is wrong" one. Make sure you direct your audience toward the questions the screenplay is asking. Offer different takes on possible answers.

If you're having trouble identifying themes in your screenplay, think of the following questions:

⇒ **What are your characters learning?** Your characters should learn something as the events of your story unfold. If no one in the movie changes at all, it might leave the audience wanting more — in a bad way — when they leave the theater.

⇒ **What influence has the protagonist's journey had on other characters?** Typically, the themes of your movie will affect your secondary characters and their storylines as well. Think about how the lessons they learn from the hero affect their actions.

⇒ **How are your characters' lives different from when the story began?** Perhaps their lives will change in a big way. Perhaps their lives will change in a small way. This change, though, however radical it may be, speaks to the heart of your story. Think about this change and the way it reflects the themes of the movie.

⇒ **How will they continue to change their lives?** As your characters move forward in their lives, where can the audience see them going? Will it be a more optimistic or pessimistic look at the future?

⇒ **What are the parallels between the narrative of the protagonist and those of the secondary characters?** There might be a natural thematic similarity between the hero's journey and the events that happen to the other characters.

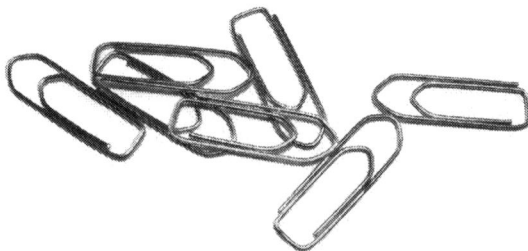

Put a twist on it

If you're struggling to identify your movie's theme, think about its core message. Your central idea is probably just a slight variation of an older one. Check out a few common themes you might run into, and think about some ways to twist them enough for yours to stand on its own.

Love conquers all

This is the most enduring of all themes — the one at the center of countless big-screen blockbusters. In the movies, even in the most mortifying of situations — whether it's meeting your in-laws in *Meet the Parents* (2000) or saving the planet in *Interstellar* (2014) — love will prevail.

A good love story doesn't have to be strictly about romantic relationships. It can be about the love of a parent for his or her children (*Finding Nemo*), the love of a family for its dog [*Marley and Me* (2008)], or the love of a person for their hometown [*Good Will Hunting* (1997)]. If it is well-written and thought-out, even the most cynical audiences can enjoy a good love story.

Good over evil

Just as love often proves more powerful than hate, good typically triumphs over evil. There are plenty examples of this, and I'm sure five just popped into your head instantly. Think of the *Harry Potter* movies, *Independence Day*, *The Avengers*, *Star Wars*, the *Lord of the Rings* trilogy, and every James Bond movie.

David vs. Goliath

Everybody likes to root for the underdog, the unlikely hero who beats the odds. Countless sports movies meet this bill, including *Rudy* (1993), *Miracle* (2004), the *Rocky* movies, *The Bad News*

Bears (1976), and *Happy Gilmore* (1996). Even non-sports movies, like *Limitless* (2011), *The Pursuit of Happyness* (2006), and *21* (2008) are effectively underdog stories.

Be careful what you wish for

Many movies feature characters getting something they deeply desire, only to find it to be not so great. This can go in many directions, like *Bruce Almighty* (2003), where an ordinary man gets to play God, or something like *13 Going on 30* (2004) or *Big* (1988), where young people are rushing to grow up. Movies like *Freaky Friday* (2003) or *The Change-Up* (2011) also show that the grass is not always greener on the other side.

Highlighting the theme

If you are unsure whether the theme of your movie will stand out to the audience, consider adding a subplot to reinforce the theme or changing an existing subplot to highlight it. You might even have a character reiterate the theme through their dialogue. However, you should be careful with this approach, because you don't want to be heavy-handed and beat your audience over the head with your message.

Theme and endings for individual characters

Even if you're trying to reinforce the theme of your movie in its subplots, you do not need to end every character's story in the same way. Maybe your hero will get exactly what he or she wants while your secondary characters don't. Similarly, your characters don't have to fail just because the protagonist does. Either way, you can make all of your stories line up with the overall theme, whether everyone fits with some kind of thesis statement or provides differing answers to a big thematic question.

For example, if your hero is a cheater, and the theme you're going for is "cheaters never prosper," the hero won't get a happy ending. But secondary characters can still hold to their morals and get happy endings of their own. At the same time, if your theme is "why do cheaters sometimes prosper?" you might have certain characters that have successful endings and certain ones that don't.

Depending on the morals of your characters and the open-endedness of your theme, there are many different places your characters can wind up.

SYMBOLIC ELEMENTS

Using symbols can be very helpful in strengthening your theme and resonating with the viewer.

For example, in the movie *Schindler's List* (1993), the girl in the red coat is a powerful symbol. The entire movie is in black and white, and she walks through the streets wearing a red coat, with Schindler not paying her much attention. She winds up making Schindler recognize his indifference toward the war and brings the death and horror of it to the forefront of his mind. She is often seen as a symbol for the blind eye the rest of the world turned toward the Holocaust as it was happening.

Think about different color and visual elements you can use to emphasize certain parts of your script. Give the audience a visual representation to drive your theme home, and help them understand certain parts of your message. You can use artifacts in your character's house, personal effects like jewelry, or a car. Think of ways to make everyday items distinct, meaningful, or attention-grabbing.

Even today, the leg lamp from *A Christmas Story* (1983) is resonant as an iconic Christmas-themed novelty item. "It's a Major Award!"

CASE STUDY: THE DO'S AND DON'TS OF TABLE READS

Annika Hylmo
Writer and script consultant
www.annikahylmo.com

A table read is a staple of Hollywood pre-production. It's an opportunity to hear your movie performed by actors without doing a full production. The actors will sit around a table and read the script from beginning to end without stopping. The writers, directors, and producers will sit to the side and listen. Afterwards, you can have a discussion about the story and get notes to consider when making adjustments to your screenplay or doing another full rewrite.

Here are some do's and don'ts to think about when you have yours:

DO

Plan

Plan ahead. Give yourself about two weeks to get your cast together and to get everything in order.

Find a space to hold your table read where you will not be interrupted. There should be enough seats for everyone in the cast to sit close together without being uncomfortable. If you have a small audience, seat them away from the actors.

Get healthy snacks and water for everyone. Make sure that all of your actors have a glass or bottle of water within reach during the reading of the script.

Cast your actors

Ask people who are used to acting to read the parts in your script. You might find them in an acting class at school or at a community theater.

Try to cast actors that resemble the parts that you wrote. GRANDMOTHER LOLA, 65, is better read by an actress who is around that age than by someone who is 15.

Confirm with everyone close to the date so they remember to come.

Print scripts and feedback forms

Print out copies of the script for all of your actors. Even if you send it to them in advance, someone will forget to bring their copy on the actual day.

Provide plenty of pens and highlighters so that your actors can mark up their scripts.

Create a feedback form with questions so that everyone can give you notes afterwards. The best questions to ask are often the simplest — what is this story about? Who is the protagonist? Who is the antagonist? What was confusing about the story? Stick to a few questions, and ask everyone in the room to fill it out.

Direct, but only a little

Plan where you want your actors to sit. The two best friends in your story might sit together, and you might want your enemies to sit further away.

Give a few directions to your actors, ask them if they have any questions, then let them do their work. Trust them to act.

Get the information you need

Time the reading so you know approximately how long your movie will be when it's been produced.

Leave time for a short discussion afterward. Let everyone fill out your feedback forms first, then listen to what they have to say. Ask for clarification if you need to.

DON'T

Invite too many people

A table read can have a couple of people who are there to listen, but it's not a staged play. Stick to people who see a lot of movies, because they will have more to compare your story with.

Get in the way of your actors

Trust them to do their job. Don't interrupt the performance or stop it halfway. The purpose of a table read is to hear it in its entirety.

Expect everyone to love your story

Some will, some won't. Don't argue with anyone's ideas or opinions or try to explain plot points that are really confusing to people. Instead, ask questions to help you understand why people were confused and what they were confused about so you can address it in your next draft.

Make promises you can't keep

It's easy to get excited about your project and to make promises that you will regret later. For example, don't promise to give someone a part in your movie if you are not 110% certain that will work out.

DO

Have fun!
APPLAUD everyone's efforts after the reading! Thank everyone for participating!

Annika Hylmo is a secret-weapon story consultant who works with award-winning Hollywood screenwriters to help make their stories fantastic. She also writes her own screenplays about strong teen girls and women who make a difference in the world. Check out her website to learn what projects are about to go into production.

CHAPTER 7:

LOOK LIKE A PRO – FORMATTING AND REVISIONS

The first time you write the words of your script should not be the last time you see them. Writing a script is not like writing a book report for school. You have to go back and revise, revise, and revise some more. When you start showing people your script, it needs to be in its best possible form. Make the writing and dialogue as dynamic and sparkling as possible, and make sure that everything is formatted correctly and proofread carefully. Your script needs to be up to professional standards. If it's improperly formatted and full of grammatical errors, you will be dismissed as an amateur right off the bat. Give yourself every advantage over lazy scriptwriters that you possibly can.

Computers can't detect contextual errors, so your spell-checker won't catch everything. Make sure character names and places are consistent throughout. Check any facts in your story. If your script looks professional and you take the time to do your research, you will, at the very least, look like someone who knows what you're doing. That gives you a chance to be judged solely on your storytelling merit.

This chapter will cover screenwriting software, formatting, getting feedback, and rewriting to help you ensure you deliver your screenplay for review in the best condition possible.

SCREENWRITING SOFTWARE

You might think screenwriting software is an unnecessary purchase since you can just use Microsoft® Word or a different word processor to build your screenplay. However, constantly switching your formatting every time you go from dialogue to slug line or vice versa can be exhausting and can take away from time you could be spending writing. If you have a limited amount of time to write every day, screenwriting software can make you much more efficient and productive overall.

There are several different programs available for screenwriting. Final Draft (~$250, **www.finaldraft.com**) is the "industry standard" and probably the best-known screenwriting program in the United States. While not quite as popular, Movie Magic Screenwriter is Final Draft's biggest competition and offers similar functions (~$250, available in several online stores). Both programs feature templates for movie scripts, as well as a function where the computer can read your script out loud to you. For writers who work on a team, both programs offer file sharing via real-time internet. Celtx Plus (~$0−$20/ month, **www.celtx.com**), Adobe Story (~$10/month on its own, **www.story.adobe.com)**, and Fade In (~$50, **www.fadeinpro.com**) are just some of the many other kinds of screenwriting software available to you.

Trust me: being organized and having screenwriting software to guide you through the process will make your life a lot easier.

FORMATTING

Your completed screenplay should have a cover page with the name of your script and "a screenplay by [your name]" or "written by [your name]" on it. In the bottom right-hand corner, list your contact details (if you have representation, you can list your representation's contact details in that corner).

You should not write a date anywhere on your script, as you do not want your readers to think the script is really old. This is not because taking your time to finish from the day you dated your script is bad. It is simply because the date might give readers the impression that no one has bought your script yet because it isn't good. In other words, if there is an old date on the cover, your reader might assume that you have only sent him or her the script after many others have turned it down.

Similarly, do not number your drafts (i.e. first draft, second draft, etc.). It is unnecessary and only serves to clutter your title page. And again, it can only create bad first impressions. Seeing "first draft" on your script might convince readers you haven't done any work to improve it. Conversely, if it says "sixth draft," your reader might think your script required so much tinkering that it can't be good.

Number the pages, but not the acts or scenes. You should leave open the possibility to move those things around at a later point.

The accepted font for screenplays is Courier or Courier New, 12 point. All professional screenwriters use this font, and in this format, one typed page typically translates to about one minute of screen time. To a trained eye, using another font or changing the size will mark you as an amateur. Leave the right margin at the default setting, and set the left margin at 1.5 inches. Dialogue should be centered, with the character's name above the lines he or she speaks, like this:

```
                    JOHN
          I made this for you.
```

Scene descriptions should be aligned left and single-spaced.

```
John stands in front of Nicole. He carries
a large shoulder bag and a bouquet of
roses. Roger stands just behind him.
```

Character names are capitalized only as they first appear, above a line of dialogue that they will speak.

```
ROGER PETERSON, 44, is a blond All-American,
built like a linebacker but smart as a whip.
```

In a novel, the author has the choice of present or past tense. But in film, everything is happening as your characters go along, so the script needs to be in present tense. Scene descriptions and actions need to be kept as concise and to-the-point as possible.

If you interrupt a character's speech with an action, indicate it in parentheses, as long as the same character is doing the action.

```
                    JOHN
            I made this for you.

        (reaches into his bag)

            Here.
```

If someone else is doing the action, indicate this on the left-hand side, as you would a scene description.

```
                    JOHN
            I made this for you.

    Roger hands him the box.

                    JOHN
                (continues)

            Here.
```

In the movie business, the heading, or line that describes and sets up the scene, is known as the slug line. It abbreviates the camera location of exterior or interior, lists the location of the scene, and says when the scene is taking place. The slug line should be written in all caps.

FEEDBACK

Finishing a screenplay is an amazing achievement, and you have a right to be proud of the work that you've done. Regardless of what happens after this moment, you have proven your discipline and creativity. But your work is far from done.

Once you are happy with your script overall, put the whole thing away. Hide it in a dark corner of your closet. Lock it in a safe. Bury it in your backyard. Mentally, get yourself as far away from your script as you can for about two weeks. If you have ideas about improving it during this time, you should definitely write them down, but try to stay away from the script until your mandated break time is over. When you bring your script back out, you should be able to view it with a fresh pair of eyes. Make all the adjustments and improvements that you find necessary.

Now it's time to see what others think of your screenplay. People who weren't involved in the writing process will be able to give you a fresh perspective on what's working and what isn't. This will help you determine which parts are worth tinkering with and which aren't so that you don't get too carried away making changes.

For your first readers, print a full script and ask them to read the whole thing before offering any opinions. Do not badger them or ask for updates as they review it. Allow them enough time to finish and fully digest the script.

Opening yourself up to feedback

Brace yourself, because this part can be tough. When you work really hard on something, opening yourself up to criticism can be trying. Unfortunately, that's just part of being a writer. You have to be willing to admit mistakes and accept valid criticisms.

When getting feedback, though, you might want to consider reaching outside the friends and family bubble. People you are close to may struggle to tell you the truth because they don't want to upset you, or they might unintentionally come across as far too critical or hurtful. If you can learn how to accept and apply direct, honest feedback, that will make your writing better and prepare you for the real world where you will have to show your script to ruthless Hollywood execs and potentially even get reviewed by movie critics.

If you are really anxious about getting feedback, create a feedback sheet with questions directly related to the screenplay and the things that you feel need to work. This can help get you specific answers to things and still improve your screenplay. Try to find value and merit in all of your feedback. Remember, everyone who gives you feedback is just trying to help improve your screenplay. Be grateful for their time.

Professional feedback

When you send your screenplay out for professional evaluation, your reader will perform a service called coverage, where he or she reviews your script and provides feedback and notes. This service typically costs money, so make sure you do your due diligence and decide if it is worth it for you.

Coverage is also the term for the report a professional reader at a studio would prepare on a newly submitted script. This report is what an agent will review before attempting to read an entire script. The reader will give the script a recommendation: pass (meaning a rejection) or consider (meaning the script is worth a look). Traditionally, the coverage review contains a synopsis of the movie's plot, as well as an opinion on several aspects of the script. Dialogue, character development, and plot structure are all given a rating.

Taylor Gaines
42, Challenge Drive
Creativity, FL

Getting Out of Grossville
a screenplay by Taylor Gaines

Consider

If you hire a script consultant, expect to pay per page to receive a commentary on your script. The consultant might suggest broad changes for the overall project or offer more specific ideas for particular sections of the script that need work. You can do an online search for any decent script consultant to get a sense of his or her reputation.

REWRITING

After getting feedback on your script, you might need to undertake a rewrite. A rewrite can be a total restart, known as a Page One rewrite, or it can just consist of adjustments to portions of the script. After finishing a first draft, a rewrite might be the last thing you want to deal with. Even having to rewrite a portion of a script can be really frustrating. But if the script isn't completely working, you owe it to yourself to try something new. Whether you are doing a full or partial rewrite, do not be afraid to try again.

ASK THE EXPERTS: "By the time I am nearing the end of a story, the first part will have been reread and altered and corrected at least one hundred and fifty times. I am suspicious of both facility and speed. Good writing is essentially rewriting. I am positive of this."
   – Roald Dahl, 20th century novelist, short story writer, and poet

If you only rewrite part of your script, be very careful about making sure it still fits into the larger framework of the story. After creating your new section, read it over again along with the sections just before and after it. Everything still needs to hold together and make sense big-picture.

ASK THE EXPERTS: "Throw up into your typewriter every morning. Clean up every noon."
    — Raymond Chandler, British-American novelist and screenwriter

If you have decided to rewrite, not because things don't make sense but because the story simply isn't interesting, go back and look at each scene to see where it is losing steam. Start with the most important ones: the opening, the ending, the climax, the midpoint, and the major plot points. If these scenes are not popping off the page, consider why. Trust your instincts. Remember, it's easier to fix things in small increments than in large blocks. As you read and analyze each scene, assess how it contributes to the primary story. Every scene has to tell the audience something about the journey, the motivations behind it, and the aspirations that fuel it.

ASK THE EXPERTS: "Writing and rewriting are a constant search for what it is one is saying."
    — John Updike, prolific novelist, poet, and short story writer

If you are overwhelmed, read your script all the way through once without stopping to analyze it. Get a sense of the big picture. Then, read it again, taking the time to make notes on each scene and what needs to happen for each one to work, either by hand or in a word processor. Try to categorize the problem in each scene. Is the problem the content itself, the fact that not enough is happening, or that the style of writing is too dense?

Here are a few things you can try if you feel like not enough is happening over the course of your story:

➡ Try condensing the events of your script and making the story more concise. Make things happen faster. See what you can cut out of your first 10 pages. Don't leave the audience any time to get bored. Introduce only the things that absolutely need to be there. Cut your story down to its simplest form, and see if it still holds your interest.

➡ Add more complications. This doesn't mean to make your story unnecessarily longer or more confusing. This simply means you should make your hero work harder for what he or she wants. If the second act is dragging, this can be a good way to try to solve your problems. Remember, the hero needs to fight for what he or she wants for the audience to be satisfied with the result.

➡ Does each scene have a strong conflict running through it? If a scene falls flat, it might be because the conflict is not good enough. Perhaps there is not enough at stake or the conflict is unclear. Look at the points that you listed on your index card for each scene. Is the essence of each scene coming through in the finished product? Is each character's motivation apparent?

➡ Add more distinctive and interesting details to the script. Move scenes to more exciting locations. Change up situations to see what it brings out of your characters. Add something symbolic to fill your scene with meaning. Make the story distinctly your story and the characters distinctly your characters.

If your writing seems to be too dense and full of exposition, find things that you can show rather than tell the audience. Ask yourself in each scene:

- How can you show the viewer what location you are in? Instead of wasting words explaining where characters are and why, see if you can incorporate a sign, flyer, or billboard that shows the audience where they are. Sometimes, the place can be recognizable without you having to say anything specifically. You don't have to say, "I have to call you back. I'm at my kid's school." Instead, you can just show your protagonist standing in a hallway outside of a classroom full of children's artwork, and the protagonist's child can run by. Your audience will probably figure it out.

- If your movie is a comedy, how can you add physical comedy to a scene? Instead of telling all of your jokes with dialogue, show some with action. Physical comedy doesn't have to be slapstick. It can be one person dressed wrongly for a fancy occasion or the straight face of a character while something intensely funny is happening that they can't afford to laugh at. Physical jokes do not have to be gross or cheap, either. They can come from funny, awkward moments that feel true to life.

- Hack away at unnecessary words. Remember, there is no time for flowery prose and description in a screenplay.

- Trust your actors. You might think they need words to convey their feelings, but talented actors can convey their characters' emotions in many ways. It is their craft. You don't need to overwrite emotions. For example:

```
Jesse enters the kitchen confidently.

                    JESSE
              Honey, I'm home!

Jesse walks through the kitchen, turning his head
from left to right, looking around each doorway to
see if she is hiding. Shaking his head, he walks
up to the dining table and reads the note on it.


                    JESSE
                  No! No!


He shakes his head and finally lays it between his
hands on the table, tears running down his face.
```

Unlike the example above, this simpler version allows more room
for creative interpretation:

```
Jesse enters the kitchen smiling.

                    JESSE
              Honey, I'm home!

Jesse looks around in the kitchen, walks to
the dining table, and reads the note on it.

                    JESSE
                  No! No!

He begins to break down.
```

The actor playing Jesse will want to have the opportunity to interpret
the dialogue. Part of the actor's job is to take the material and make
it his or her own. A good screenwriter allows actors to make choices
and really play with their characters.

CASE STUDY: THREE THINGS TO CONSIDER BEFORE WRITING A SCREENPLAY

Haik Kocharian
Writer, Director, and Producer
www.haikkocharian.com
Twitter: @HKocharia

The screenplay writing process is riddled with challenges. You have to develop, formulate, and refine the story. You have to make sure you have proper formatting, that you've closely proofread the text, and much more. The list of laborious and, at times, maddening tasks is long. But before you even write the first sentence, there are three issues you need to consider.

First, how do you balance success (or lack thereof) and self-esteem? Second, how do you allow your idea to reach its full potential and avoid it becoming an idea that appeared exciting at first but was never developed?

Third, and most important, understand why you want to write. The decision to write a screenplay means dedicating a good chunk of your life to an idea that might not bring you the success and recognition you desire. Before you embark on this exhilarating but risky journey, ask yourself a simple question: *Why am I doing this?*

Here is my advice on how to answer these three fundamental questions.

Focus on your voice

Don't compare, and don't compete. Let's say you're living in Los Angeles, and you have a screenwriter roommate — same age as you — who lands an agent and is offered a position on a popular television series. You're pretty happy for him, but you're also jealous of his success. Questions keep running through your head. *Why him and not me? My writing is just as good if not better than his. Why am I so unlucky?* You feel weak, insecure, and discouraged. But you should not compare yourself with him or try to compete with his success. Don't worry too much about what other people do and receive in their careers. Stay focused on your own vision, your own way of thinking. Write your story in your unique voice and focus your energy on writing the absolute best screenplay you can rather than expending your time and energy on comparing yourself to others.

Finish the first draft

Screenwriting can be a brutal and difficult creative process. This is particularly true when writing the first draft. Everything feels off. The characters appear flat and underdeveloped, the dialogue is a disaster, and the storyline is full of holes. At times, you feel as if you are unable to put a single sentence on the page. A terrifying doubt starts to linger: *Is the story good enough?* Perhaps your doubts are justified, and the story isn't very good. But maybe it's a diamond in the rough. You can only settle this question by finishing your first draft. Make your points, even if they aren't yet well-defined, and put all of your thoughts and ideas in writing. Only after you have finished your first draft will you be able to assess the story's potential.

Love what you do

This is perhaps the most important part. You should write screen-plays because you have a story to tell, one that has inspired you and become a part of you. Write bravely, with vigor and excitement. Don't be afraid to be original and take risks. We all seek recognition and success as a screenwriter. If you write with passion and determination, success will follow.

Haik Kocharian is a screenwriter, director, producer, fine arts photographer, and singer-songwriter. Mr. Kocharian is the writer and director of the award-winning feature film, "Please be Normal."

CHAPTER 8:

BECOME A MARKETING EXPERT

Writing is a creative pursuit, and after all the hard work it takes to finish your screenplay, it might be easy to forget about the important business side of getting it made. Here's the process in a nutshell: A writer writes a script. An agent sells that script. Publicists build up some buzz around it. Then, producers put up the money to get it made.

As a young screenwriter, you may have to do more than one of these jobs at once. At the beginning, you are your only advocate. It is *your* job to find other advocates for your screenplay and convince people that it deserves to get made.

Getting your screenplay sold is going to be the hardest part of the journey, especially as a first-time writer. If you don't have any contacts in the industry, even getting an agent to look at your screenplay is going to be really tough. Competition is fierce, and many other writers are trying to get their movies made, too.

Learning how to handle rejection and maintaining your drive is going to be crucial if you want to make it. The time that passes between when you start trying to sell and actually manage to sell a script can be long. How many times do you think you could get rejected before you want to give up? Alright, now double that number. It will take at least that many attempts to get your script sold.

COPYRIGHT

Before you can really begin searching for an agent to try to sell your script, you need to take a few steps to protect yourself. Your script is your intellectual property. As its creator, you alone have exclusive rights to it. However, you should still copyright your work. Copyrighting is important, because it legally protects your intellectual property and registers the date on which you finished it.

Under the law, your work belongs to you the moment you create it. But if you should ever need to prove in a court of law that you created it by a certain date, the copyright will benefit you greatly.

A copyright grants you sole rights to your work, rights that include creating derivative works, performing the work, and making copies of the work itself. If you are wondering, a derivative work is one that borrows so heavily from the original in that it cannot be considered original itself. No can perform any of the above actions without first getting your permission and compensating you. It is unlikely you will run into copyright problems, but a copyright is a pretty easy and affordable way to protect yourself.

Copyrights through the U.S. Copyright Office

To copyright your work, you need to register your intellectual property with the U.S. Copyright Office. Although your work is protected from the moment you created it, the date can be very hard to prove. Typically, the official date that legal entities go by is the date that the copyright office grants your application. You will get a certificate of registration in the mail that shows this date. Copyright protection lasts until 70 years after your death.

The actual process of obtaining your copyright is fairly simple. There a few different ways you can do it. You can apply for a copyright online at the U.S. Copyright Office website, **www.copyright. gov**. This carries a lower fee and has a faster processing time than other options. The online method also allows you to track the progress of your submission. The processing time for a copyright application can be long, and if you apply by mail, you will have no idea how things are progressing. To process your application online, complete the form, pay the $35 fee, and upload a copy of your work.

If you really want to mail your forms, the copyright office recommends you print and use their form, which contains a barcode the office can use to scan it. The copyright application is then processed much faster than if you complete all the forms by hand. This form can be printed from their website and mailed in with your script and a $50 filing fee. You can also do things the really old-fashioned way and fill out all your forms by hand and mail them in. The processing time for this type of submission can be up to four or five months.

> **FAST FACT:** You cannot copyright an idea. You can only copyright the actual production of an idea.

Registering your script with the WGA

The Writers Guild of America, or WGA, also offers you the ability to register your script. The guild is split into East and West, with offices in Los Angeles and New York. To join, you need to do work for a company that the Guild recognizes. By working for a recognized company, you earn units with the guild based on the amount of work you do. Once you obtain a certain number of units, you can join as an associate member, and eventually, a current member.

You do not need to be a WGA member to register your script. This is a separate service that the guild provides. Once registered, you are offered five years of protection (this is similar to a copyright but does not replace it). To register your script, pay the registration fee and upload the document to the WGA website (**www.wga.org** or **www.wgaeast.org**). The fee to register is $20 for non-members. The work is then considered deposited with the WGA. Imagine you are locking your script away in a room somewhere for safe-keeping. This is effectively what you are doing. If you submit a hard copy, it will quite literally be placed somewhere under lock and key, and only the registered writer can access it or request copies. You can also register treatments, idea outlines, and drafts with the WGA.

Once your script is protected under the law, you can start preparing to sell it.

RESEARCHING THE MARKET

To get your script sold, you are going to have to do a different kind of research and writing than you're used to. You need to research agents, industry contacts, contests, and other possible existing contacts — things you might be able to use to get your script submitted. This might not be as creative of a process as writing the script, but it's just as important. You could write the best script in the world, but if you don't make a strong effort in your sales pitch, it might never get seen.

Knowing how to target the market when selling your work is crucial. Try to familiarize yourself with the kinds of deals that have recently been made in Hollywood to get a sense of the current climate and to make your pitch more effective.

Here are some factors you should look at when trying to determine the market for your script:

➡ **Recent films.** It can take a long time for a script to go from its inception to its actual release date. Say you are finishing your script when you discover that a movie nearly identical to yours is about to be released by a major studio. This doesn't mean you can't sell your script. Research the similar movie, and highlight the ways your script is different.

➡ **Recent hits.** The movie industry is often slow-moving. If there are successful movies with similar demographics to yours, you might want to try to take advantage of that when selling your script. The successful movie will give you a good idea of how marketable yours might be.

➡ **Recent sales.** Publications like *Variety, Deadline,* and *The Hollywood Reporter* frequently report on the latest Hollywood news and deals and are available in print and online. Keep up with publications like these to get an idea of what Hollywood is currently spending its money on. Use this knowledge to your advantage when pitching and selling your script.

➡ **Recent technology.** If you are aspiring to be a filmmaker as well as a writer, you might not even need to worry about selling your script. You can make it happen yourself. Recruit local actors, camera operators, and editors to help with the project. Computer animation is easier to use, and in some cases, cheaper than ever before. If you live near a school that offers a film curriculum, consider taking some classes or recruiting someone to make a student film with your script.

THE SALE PROCESS

The conventional path to getting a script sold starts with an agent. The first thing you will do is try to get an agent to represent you and your script. The agent will then try to sell your script to a studio. You can also try to sell the script directly to the studio, using a manager or lawyer as your way in. Screenwriting contests abound as well. Some offer cash prizes, and others offer simple exposure and access to people in the industry.

To sell your screenplay, there are different kinds of documents, treatments, outlines, and sales pitches you need to prepare. Selling a script is effectively just selling yourself: your talent as a writer, your proofreading skills, and the genius idea that has driven you this far. Get ready to talk more about yourself and your work than you ever have.

The agent

One thing that could help you as you try to sell yourself is an agent. Having an agent who will champion your work is a big advantage as you go through the process of trying to get your script sold. Good agents have connections that can get your script in the hands of people with the power to get it made. Most studios will probably throw your script into the trash if you send it to them unsolicited, so having an agent who can place it directly into their hands will greatly increase your chances of getting it seen.

Seeking an agent can be a long process. You will have to be tenacious and persistent to get noticed. When submitting a script to an agent, make sure you do things the way he or she requests so that your submission doesn't get denied or sent back for a small reason unrelated to your script. Along with your work, an agent is going to look at your cover/query letter to see how you communicate professionally. He or she will check to see that your script's formatting is up to industry standards. Remember, he or she will not take you on as a client if doing so would reflect badly on his or her agency.

If you're doing your research and keeping up with trade publications, you might be familiar with some of Hollywood's top agents. You can also research lesser-known ones online or in print. The WGA offers a full list of agents on their website (**www.wga.org/agency/agencylist.aspx**), which you can access free of charge. There are also directories in print, such as the annual *Writer's Digest Guide to Literary Agents*, edited by Chuck Sambuchino.

After compiling a list of possible agencies, research each one to see its submission process. Most agents won't read unsolicited, or not asked for, manuscripts. The amount of material this could add up to would overwhelm them. Even if you do send a screenplay to an agent — *oh, they'll love it once they start reading it*, you say — they'll probably toss it without opening it. To get an agent to read your script, you have to be invited to send one to them.

Wait, so how do you get them interested in the first place? Let's talk about query letters.

Query letters

Your query letter is effectively a one-page summary of why someone should read your screenplay. The letter needs to pique the reader's interest enough to make him or her want to read the whole script. It should touch on you, your credentials, and your qualifications. The letter should also mention your accomplishments, your experience relevant to the screenplay (i.e. "I worked in a grocery store for 20 years, so I understand this world."), and any connection you might have with the agent. The letter should not be longer than one page. Do not make the page too dense. It is important to stick to the standard format and leave some white space so the reader feels comfortable.

You should absolutely not rush this step, as it is just as important as the actual writing of your script. It is easy to make spelling and grammatical errors in electronic communication. Don't let that happen. This letter should be read over several times, by you and others, to make sure it is clear and concise and as error-free as possible. This is your one shot to make a good impression with an agent and to make them want to read your script, so make it count. If you don't make a strong impression, they will almost certainly not even look at your full script.

Here are a few tips to help you nail that nerve-wracking query letter:

- Address your letter to one specific agent rather than "to whom it may concern" or "sir or madam." This shows you took the time to research the agency.
- Check your spelling, grammar, and punctuation carefully. Spell check is not thorough enough. Some proper names won't be marked right or wrong in a standard spell check. You should manually check to ensure each instance of a name is spelled correctly. Similarly, spell check will not correct you if you spell words wrong with words that are still words, such as accidentally typing the word "good" instead of "food."
- Use business English. Regardless of the style and tone of your screenplay, this is the time to showcase yourself as a professional. The agent will see how skilled you are at different writing styles when he or she reads your screenplay.

EXAMPLE OF QUERY LETTER

Date

Bob Johnson
Johnson Agency
101 Johnson Road
Hollywood, CA 90028

Dear Mr. Johnson,

My new script *Getting Out of Grossville* is about Emma, a young woman tired of her life as a grocery store cashier, who decides to take her chance to change her fate. To escape her alcoholic mother and small town, she needs to do whatever it takes to get a manager job at the grocery store. The only thing standing between her and the extra income she needs to make her dream come true is the other candidate for the job — Emma's new boyfriend and possible love of her life. *Getting Out of Grossville* is a coming-of-age story about finding love, but ultimately, about finding yourself.

The script was chosen as Best New Script in the True North Screenplay Contest. My short fiction has also won numerous awards.

The complete script is ready and available for your review. I can be reached by phone at (123) 456-7890, e-mail at grocerystoremovie@mail.com, or by using the enclosed self-addressed stamped envelope.

Sincerely,

Author's name

Follow-up letters

This process can be incredibly discouraging to young writers. You might send your work out to 100 people and not hear anything back. You will get rejected. If you send physical queries, you might get them sent back to you without even being opened.

If you persevere, you just might get the ideal response: an agent who wants to see your whole script. You can then draft a new cover letter, thanking the agent for his or her interest. Make sure you work in a mention of the fact that the agent requested the whole script so that yours isn't mistaken for an unsolicited one and thrown to the side. Enclose a self-addressed stamped envelope for return correspondence.

Here is an example of what this second letter might look like:

Date

Bob Johnson
Johnson Agency
101 Johnson Road
Hollywood, CA 90028

Dear Mr. Johnson,

Thank you so much for your prompt response
regarding my script, *Getting Out of Grossville.*
I am enclosing the entire script as you
requested in your correspondence on [date].

As a reminder, this script details the personal
journey of Emma, a young woman tired of her
life as a grocery store cashier, who decides to
take her chance to change her fate. To escape
her alcoholic mother and small town, she needs
to do whatever it takes to get a manager job
at the grocery store. The script was chosen as
Best
New Script in the True North Screenplay
Contest. My short fiction has also won numerous
awards.

If you have any other questions or concerns, I
can be reached by phone at (123) 456-7890,
e-mail at grocerystoremovie@mail.com, or using
the enclosed self-addressed stamped envelope.
I look forward to hearing from you soon.

Sincerely,

Author's name

Entering contests

There is a small bit of controversy when it comes to screenwriting contests. Most charge a fairly affordable entry fee, usually not more than $40-50. However, some writers object to the fee, not because of its amount but because of the idea that they might have to spend money on something that won't pay off. Many readers at contests might not even know much about screenwriting and aren't going to offer any feedback. Why not spend your money on something else, such as getting an actual professional to read your script?

Screenwriting contests can also be incredibly demoralizing. You might pay your entry fee, send in your script, and never hear a thing back, especially if it's a national or international contest. But then again, the same result might come from sending your script out to agents. So what do you do? If you have a thick skin and rejection never fazes you, keep entering contests. Contests can open doors for you and can give you added credentials if you win when it comes to promoting your script to agents.

Research potential contests carefully to see if you can figure out who will actually be reading your script. Some contests, like The Scriptapalooza Screenplay Contest, do not use readers to review submissions. Rather, agents, managers, and producers all read the scripts themselves. Even if your script doesn't win any awards, analysts might decide other professionals should read your script and send it to those people.

When researching contests, you should also look into whether winners of past contests have actually found representation or sold their scripts after winning. This will give you an idea of the kind of exposure you can get from different competitions.

Chapter 8: Become a Marketing Expert

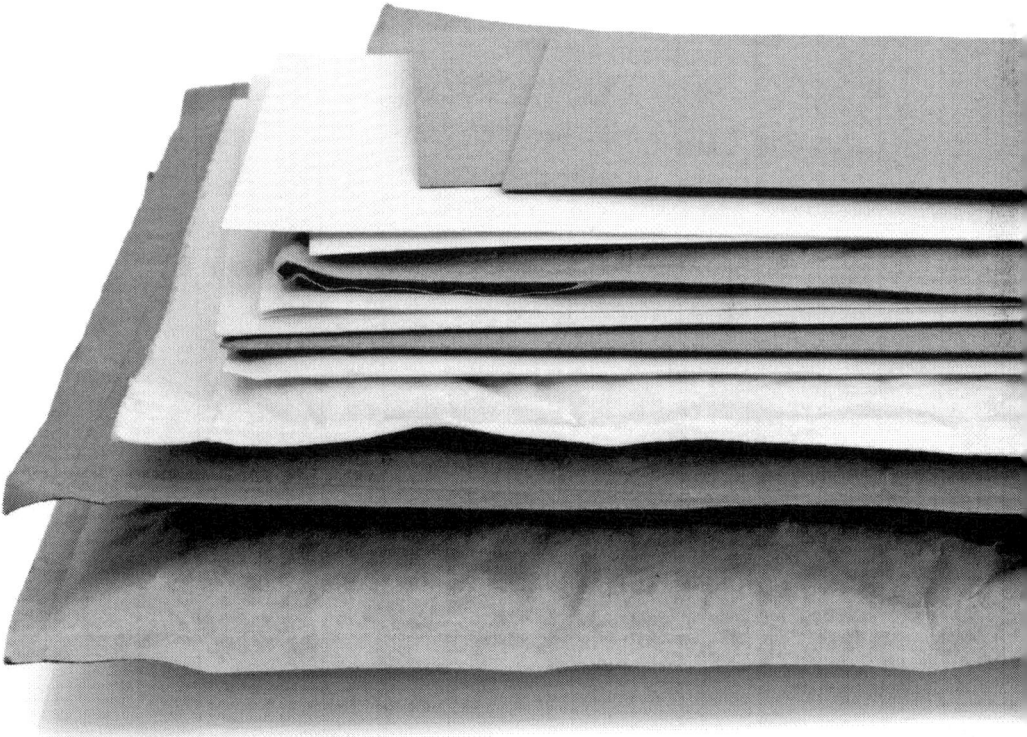

CHAPTER 9:

GET YOUR
SCRIPT ON
THE SCREEN

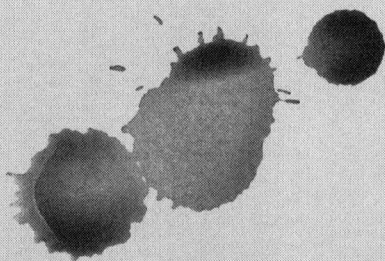

We've mentioned this already, but it bears repeating: Breaking into the Hollywood system can be really tough. Not everyone will make it big. Even though the methods we outlined in the previous chapter have proven to be the most successful, it can still take a long time, and you may still suffer countless rejections before breaking through.

If you get tired of sending query after query to unresponsive agents, there are different ways to try to get your script noticed. In this chapter, we're going to discuss networking and its benefits as well as different ways to try to get your movie made, including independent films, short films, and student films.

NETWORKING

You might think you have no connection to anyone in the movie business. But that doesn't mean you shouldn't ask around. You might have someone in your extended circle of friends, family members, neighbors, community members, church members, or co-workers who knows someone who knows someone. It's more likely than you think.

Be prepared and professional when working to expand your network. It helps other people take you seriously, and if you are professional, they will feel more confident about introducing you to their contacts. Make sure that contacts can reach you in many ways, whether by e-mail, by phone, or at a coffee shop.

Online networking
With the continually growing relevance of the internet, finding like-minded people is easier than ever. As a screenwriter, you have

to use this ease of access to your advantage. Professional networking sites such as LinkedIn™ make it easy to keep track of your network as well as potential future contacts.

Meanwhile, just because sites such as Facebook™ and Twitter™ aren't really "professional" sites, that doesn't mean they can't be useful. Once you have your own portfolio website set up, use these sites to get more exposure for yourself. The more people you get excited about your screenplay, the better the chance you have of it reaching someone who can do something with it.

You can also look through countless different sites and online communities where aspiring screenwriters like to exchange thoughts and opinions on each other's work (see appendices for more).

Setting up your own website

When setting up your personal portfolio site, it's probably a good idea to use a simple and easy-to-remember domain name. Unless your first and last names are hard to remember or spell or happen to be really common, using them is probably a good option (i.e. **www.jasonstrombone.com**). You can also incorporate your potential career field into the domain name, with something like **www.jerrythescreenwriter.com**.

If you want to set up a site just for your screenplay, you can create a domain with that title instead, i.e. **gettingoutofgrossville. com**. However, with this approach, you might have to set up a new site for every project you work on. This might not work well if you're trying to promote yourself as an individual. Basically, it's not bad to have a site for your screenplay, but you should definitely have one that focuses on you, too.

Remember to keep your site updated. This will keep readers coming back and ensure that people considering you for work don't stumble upon an unused and outdated web page. Make sure your site's URL is prominently displayed on all of your social media profiles so people can find it easily.

If you have experience with coding and web design, feel free to take a crack at making your site yourself. If you don't, there are many hosting providers that offer templates you can use to make a perfectly useful site.

A great site to look at for inspiration is **www.johnaugust.com**. It promotes screenwriter John August but also offers news about screenwriting, information about his projects, and other information on a streamlined, clean-looking site.

Now you've written your script, made your site, and reached out to countless agents. What if you just wanted to get your movie made now? Good news. You have a few options.

INDEPENDENT FILMS

Movies that are produced without the typical financial backing of the Hollywood studio system are usually referred to as independent films. The name comes from the idea that these filmmakers are "independent" of the major film studio system. The roots of this system trace back to the days when filmmakers who used studio financing were restricted by a certain code and way of doing things. If artists wanted to really express themselves and do something less creatively restricting or more "indecent" or "suggestive," they had to go outside of the studio system to find funding. Similarly, filmmakers who wanted to tell stories with ambiguous endings or make horror and science fiction typically weren't supported in the studio system.

These days, the phrase "independent film" has less to do with the content and more to do with the lower cost and easier accessibility of filmmaking equipment.

Independent films can still make money. Many independent films have won festivals, and as a result, they have seen way more press attention and become hits. Since they carry smaller costs, studios could potentially purchase them cheaply and make a profit.

FAST FACT: The highest-grossing independent movie of all-time is Mel Gibson's The Passion of the Christ (2004), which he self-financed. It made $611.9 million worldwide.

Alternate ways to pitch your movie

If you're sick and tired of trying to break in to the studio system, you can try to turn to independent production companies. However, independent studios are often so small that they only produce one or two films per year. Still, this type of company might be more likely to review an unsolicited manuscript than a big Hollywood studio. For instance, Stars North (**www.starsnorth.com**) in Orlando is an independent movie company that accepts unsolicited manuscripts for short and feature-length films. All they ask is that your work be copyrighted and properly registered with the WGA. Luckily for you, we discussed how to do both of those things earlier, so I hope you paid attention!

Maybe you're sick and tired of sending your script to people and never hearing back. Maybe you just want feedback. You can look into attending events designed for aspiring screenwriters to pitch their projects, often called "pitch fests." These events are frequently held in Los Angeles, sometimes as part of a larger conference or event. They do often cost a lot of money to attend, and there is no guarantee they can help you move your career forward. Still, there won't be many opportunities to get to pitch to a room full of development executives, producers, and other industry insiders. They will typically hear your five-minute pitch in small groups, and if they're interested, they might request that you send your script to them.

In any case, if you get an opportunity to pitch your movie to a producer or an agent, practice as much as possible before the event. Keep the pitch as short as possible, preferably under two minutes. If you can get it down to one, that's even better. Try to present the major, attention-grabbing aspects of your movie. Who is the story about? What is important to know about the characters? What journey will the movie follow them on? Why should the audience care?

If you're asked for a longer pitch, don't exceed 10 minutes. Begin with the logline and summarize the action of the film. This type of pitch is completely different, and there are many books and guides out there to help you structure this kind of longer pitch.

SHORT FILMS

The phrase "short film" doesn't come with any strict rules attached. Lengths of short films can vary wildly, anywhere from about 10 to 40 minutes. For Oscar consideration, a short film must be 40 minutes or less.

A short film is cheaper and, well, shorter, which gives anyone interested in your work a chance to see a narrative and characters you have created. It also gives you something else to add to your query letters when listing your previous work.

If you have a longer script written, you might consider choosing a few scenes from it and creating a short film out of those scenes. You could make the ending ambiguous so that someone might be compelled to want to see the full, feature version.

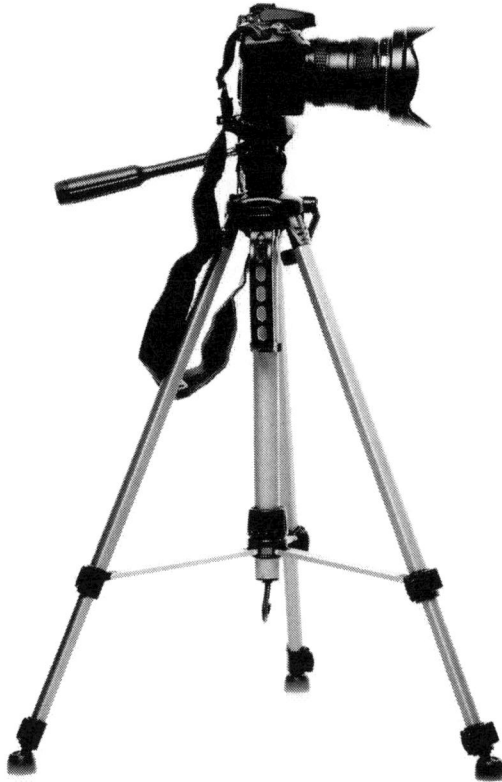

You may already own equipment good enough to produce a short film. If you have a digital camera, you can most likely take video. Movies have even been made on the iPhone. You can then download a free program to edit movie clips, such as iMovie or Windows Movie Maker. You could also purchase higher-end video editing software, but you can do the basics with the ones listed here.

Some writers try to use social media to garner buzz for their short films, whether they are uploading them to YouTube or trying to gain a following on Twitter. It might take a lucky break and a viral video or two, but posting short films online can help you build a reputation.

STUDENT FILMS

Another approach you could take is to enroll yourself in film classes. Do some research to figure out which schools in your area are best and which fit into your price range well. Film school will teach you everything you need to know about the historical and technical aspects of filmmaking. Still, it may not be the right approach for everyone. Maybe you just want to learn how to do better camera work or editing. There's a chance that classes on these things are offered at a local community college or technical school that specializes in filmmaking.

Classes are beneficial, because they offer you instruction and feedback every step of the way, and they will force you to learn how to work collaboratively.

If you aren't interested in taking classes, you can always try to work with a student. They might be able to provide knowledge about the technical aspects of filmmaking that you are unfamiliar with. Post an ad on Craigslist or on a campus message board to see if someone is interested in working with you.

CONCLUSION

So, why do you want to try screenwriting? Has your idea just been eating away at you, and you feel compelled to get it on paper? Maybe you just want a new hobby. Maybe you want to be a star. Maybe you have a passion for writing.

Whatever the reason, you need to remember that succeeding at screenwriting depends on more than your ability to write a screenplay, and frankly, on more than just talent. Marketing, networking, legwork, and luck are all large factors when it comes to whether your screenplay will ever get looked at, let alone made into a film. If you possess the magical combination of talent, persistence, and luck that it takes to make it as a screenwriter, you might just find a new, profitable career.

Keep in mind, though, finishing a script is a major accomplishment, even if it never gets made. It is impressive that you had the drive to finish your screenplay, the resilience to edit even when you didn't want to, and the resolve to re-write and cut sections that you poured your soul into. In the end, if you did all of these things, you should be proud of yourself.

Writing a screenplay is not something that can happen overnight. Writing, editing, polishing, and sending out a screenplay for sale is a long-term project. You can't know how this endeavor will turn out when you start writing, but I guarantee you nothing will happen if you don't write anything at all.

Who knows if you'll make it? No one can say. What matters is that you enjoy the journey. If you have a story that you want to tell, a story that's important to you, the best you can do is sit down and write it.

BIBLIOGRAPHY

McCabe, John. "6 Best Screenwriting Software Options." *Videomaker*. January (2016). 13 July 2015. Web.

Mohr, Ian. "Production Costs Climb." *Variety*. Variety 411, 07 Mar. 2007. Web.

Samaroo, Melissa. *The Complete Guide to Writing a Successful Screenplay: Everything You Need to Know to Write and Sell a Winning Script*. Ocala, FL: Atlantic Group, 2015. Print.

Siegemund-Broka, Austin, and Paul Bond. "Hollywood Salaries Revealed: Who Makes What on the Lot and on Location." *The Hollywood Reporter*. The Hollywood Reporter, 2 Oct. 2015. Web.

The Writers' Guild of Great Britain. *Writing Film: A Good Practice Guide*. Rep. Writers' Guild of Great Britain, Apr. 2016. Web.

GLOSSARY

Antagonist: a person who is opposed to, struggles against, or competes with another, usually the protagonist; opponent; adversary.

Bollywood: the motion-picture industry of India, based in Bombay.

Button: a final addition to the end of a scene intended to provide levity or pique the audience's interest.

Catalyst: a person or thing that causes an event or change to occur; a driving force in work.

Climax: the highest point of action or conflict in a work.

Copyright: the exclusive right to make copies, license, and otherwise use a literary, musical, or artistic work, whether printed, audio, video, etc. Works granted such right by law on or after January 1, 1978, are protected for the lifetime of the author or creator and for a period of 70 years after his or her death.

Coverage: the analysis and grading of screenplays, often part of the "script development" department of a production company. Also the term for the actual written report that analyzes the script being either passed on or considered.

Deus ex machina: any artificial or improbable device resolving the difficulties of a plot.

Easter eggs: hidden messages or hints in a work.

Exposition: background information in a work; prior plot events or historical context.

Greek chorus: a group of people in a classical Greek play designed to formulate, express, and comment on the moral issues raised by the dramatic action or to express emotions appropriate to each stage of the dramatic action.

Heist Movie: a movie involving some sort of planned robbery or act of theft.

Inciting Incident: an event that sets the plot of a book, movie, or play in motion.

MacGuffin: an element in a work that the plot is driving toward.

Montage: the process or technique of selecting, editing, and piecing together separate sections of film or scenes to form a continuous whole.

Mumblecore: a relatively new low-budget film genre where performances are emphasized as natural or improvised.

Nollywood: the motion-picture industry of Nigeria.

Page One rewrite: when a script has a strong central premise and good characters but is otherwise unusable, a different writer or team of writers might be brought on to perform this.

Protagonist: the leading character in a work, usually competing against the antagonist.

Query letter: a one-page summary trying to influence someone to read a screenplay.

Reflection (character): the voice of reason in a film.

Romance character: the character that serves as a love interest in a work.

Schadenfreude: a German term for the pleasure one gets from seeing another's misfortune.

Screenplay: the script of a movie, including acting instructions and scene directions.

Screenwriting: the art and craft of writing scripts for mass media such as feature films, television productions, or video games.

Slug line: a line of abbreviated text at the beginning of each scene in a screenplay that describes the location and time of day.

Subtext: an underlying and often distinct theme in a piece of writing or conversation.

Symbolism: the use of symbols to represent ideas or qualities.

The New French Wave: a movement in French cinema in the 1960s, led by directors such as Jean Luc Godard and François Truffaut, that abandoned traditional narrative techniques in favor of greater use of symbolism and abstraction and dealt with themes of social alienation, psychopathology, and sexual love.

Three-act structure: a model used in screenwriting that divides a fictional narrative into three parts.

Ticking clock: an element of time by which an act or event must occur, usually adding tension.

Tropes: a figurative or metaphorical use of a word or expression, usually common and easily recognized.

Unsolicited: not asked for; in this case, sending your script to an agent or production company without first contacting them.

Writers Guild: an organization of authors that is considered a labor union in the U.S.; made up of members from the east and west coast.

ADDITIONAL RESOURCES

This section gives you an idea of where to begin looking online for information on screenwriting. Though all contests and paid services listed here have been verified to be legitimate, they might not be right for your specific script. Conduct some research and make your own decision based on the subject and marketability of your script.

SAMPLE SCRIPTS

Here are some sites where you can find famous movie scripts for reading and reviewing as well as classic movies to watch.

Simply Scripts
www.simplyscripts.com

Drew's Script-O-Rama
www.script-o-rama.com

The Internet Movie Script Database
www.imsdb.com

ABOUT SCREENWRITING

These sites talk about the process and craft of screenwriting.

Screenwriters Utopia
www.screenwritersutopia.com

Cinestory

A nonprofit organization that offers fellowships, a contest, and re-sources for screenwriters.

www.cinestory.org

The Writers Store

An online store that offers resources for writers and filmmakers.

www.writersstore.com

HOLLYWOOD AND THE BUSINESS

These websites and organizations list the most recent deals and contests for screenwriters in Hollywood.

Done Deal Professional

Reports on the latest deals in Hollywood and around the world; also has directories of agents and managers.

www.donedealpro.com

Scriptapalooza screenplay contest

www.scriptapalooza.com

Movie Bytes

A directory of screenwriting contests.

www.moviebytes.com

The Writers Guild Association

Association for working writers. Lots of valuable information on their site that is accessible to non-members.

www.wga.org

Talentville

A similar concept to Trigger Street Labs. Screenwriters can upload completed work for review and can review work from others.

www.talentville.com

The International Screenwriters Association

Worldwide screenwriting association. Free to join.

www.networkisa.org

WORKING SCREENWRITERS AND INDUSTRY INSIDERS

Here are some blogs and official websites of people with an inside view of Hollywood.

SydField.com

Official website of Syd Field, screenwriting guru. Offers information about Syd Field and general information for screenwriters.

www.sydfield.com

Complications Ensue

Blog of TV and Film screenwriter Alex Epstein.

http://complicationsensue.blogspot.com

Screenwriting from Iowa

Blog of Scott Smith, who details his experiences working as a screenwriter living outside of Hollywood.

http://screenwritingfromiowa.wordpress.com

John August

Official website of screenwriter John August and the Scriptnotes podcast.

www.johnaugust.com

The Bitter Script Reader

A blog by a Hollywood script reader that offers advice on scripts.

http://thebitterscriptreader.blogspot.com

Go Into The Story

Blog of Scott Meyers, screenwriting teacher and former Hollywood writer and producer.

www.gointothestory.com

DOWNLOADS

These free downloads can be useful for screenwriters.

Abode Premiere Pro

Movie making software. Download a free 30-day trial.

www.adobe.com/downloads.html

Final cut Pro

Movie editing software for Apple OS. Free 30-day trial.

www.apple.com/final-cut-pro/trial

Scrivener

Writing software for Apple OS. Free trial available.

www.literatureandlatte.com/trial.php

Join.me

A useful software for collaboration. Allows you to remotely see someone else's computer screen.

https://join.me

INDEX

A
antagonist 7, 59, 79, 108, 112, 166, 221-222, 231
arc 34, 77, 104-105, 132

B
Bollywood 6, 57-58, 221, 231

C
camera directions 43, 231
Catalyst 114, 221, 231
character development 8, 35, 81, 101, 180, 231
climax 9, 56, 119, 122-123, 151, 181, 221, 231
conflict 9, 36-37, 87-88, 130-131, 136, 182, 221, 231
contests 11, 30, 196, 198, 204, 225-226, 231, 233
convention 123, 151
copyright 2, 8, 191-193, 219

D
details 5, 20, 28-29, 57, 68, 75, 105, 129, 175, 182, 203, 228, 231
Deus ex machina 6, 52, 221, 231

E
Easter eggs 6, 54, 221, 231
exposition 9, 53, 140, 183, 221, 231

F
Field, Syd 231
foreign films 6, 56, 59, 231
formatting 10, 43-44, 141, 171, 173, 175, 186, 199, 231
French New Wave 6, 56, 231

G
genre 7, 49, 53, 71-75, 222, 232

I
independent films 11, 209, 211-212, 232
Internet Movie Script Database 43, 225, 232

L
language 7, 67-69, 75, 138, 232
likability 6, 76

M
MacGuffin 9, 149-150, 222, 232
marketing 10, 30, 71, 108, 191, 217, 232

N
narrative 50, 123, 159, 212, 221
networking 11, 209-210, 217, 232
nonfiction 5, 33-34, 232
nonverbal clues 44

O
occupation 7, 68, 232
outline 9, 21, 109, 127, 232

P
pitch 194, 210-212

Q
query letter 11, 199-201, 222, 232

R
research tools 7, 70, 232
revisions 10, 171, 232

rewriting 10, 30, 173, 180-181, 232
romance 6, 46, 71, 78, 106, 116, 149, 220

S
Schadenfreude 119, 222, 233
screenwriting contests 198, 204, 226, 233
screenwriting software 10, 173-174, 219, 233
secondary characters 8, 106, 112, 130, 160-161, 163, 233
short films 11, 30, 62, 209, 214, 233
stage directions 43, 138, 142, 233
story card 128-130, 233
structure, three-act 8-9, 109, 120, 125, 127, 223, 233
students films 233
studio system 209-210
style 6, 43, 49, 61, 71, 136, 182, 200, 233
subtext 9, 138-139, 157, 223, 233
symbols 131, 164, 223, 233

T
three-act structure 8-9, 109, 120, 125, 127, 223, 233
time period 7, 20, 43, 68-69, 233
tone 8, 94-95, 112, 118, 147, 200, 233
tropes 6, 52-53, 223, 233
twist 91, 119, 151, 159

V
voice 9, 14, 59, 80, 91, 106, 135-136, 141, 187, 222, 233

AUTHOR BIO

Taylor Gaines, a recent cum laude graduate from the College of Journalism & Communications at the University of Florida, is a writer and editor. His work has appeared in *The Gainesville Sun, Hooked on Hockey Magazine, Gainesville Scene, Sports Talk Florida,* and more. He has been a host of a weekly television podcast, The Fauxworthy Podcast, since 2015. He particularly enjoys writing about television, movies, and hockey but loves anything that makes for a good story.

Made in the USA
Columbia, SC
24 August 2019